SECRETS OF A CREATIVITY COACH

Eric Maisel

LEADERS IN GLOBAL PUBLISHING

Published by Motivational Press, Inc.
2360 Corporate Circle
Suite 400
Henderson, NV 89074
www.MotivationalPress.com

Manufactured in the United States of America.

ISBN: 978-1-62865-052-5

NONFICTION

Affirmations for Artists

The Art of the Book Proposal

The Atheist's Way

Become a Creativity Coach Now!

Brainstorm

Coaching the Artist Within

Creative Recovery

The Creativity Book

Creativity for Life

Deep Writing

Everyday You

Fearless Creating

A Life in the Arts

Living the Writer's Life

Making Your Creative Mark

Mastering Creative Anxiety

Natural Psychology

Performance Anxiety

The Power of Sleep Thinking

Rethinking Depression

Sleep Thinking

Ten Zen Seconds

Toxic Criticism

20 Communication Tips at Work

20 Communication Tips for Families

The Van Gogh Blues

What Would Your Character Do?

Why Smart People Hurt

Write Mind

A Writer's Paris

A Writer's San Francisco

A Writer's Space

FICTION

Aster Lynn

The Blackbirds of Mulhouse

The Black Narc

Dismay

The Fretful Dancer

The Kingston Papers

Murder in Berlin

New Israel

JOURNALS

Artists Speak

Writers and Artists on Devotion

Writers and Artists on Love

MEDITATION DECKS

Everyday Calm

Everyday Creative

Everyday Smart

For Ann, thirty-six years into this adventure

CONTENTS

INTRODUCTION

I've been coaching creative and performing artists for more than thirty years. I've worked with famous artists and unknown artists, young artists just starting out and octogenarian artists, full-time artists and artists who in their day jobs are lawyers, government workers, therapists, and blacksmiths. My clients live in the United States, Canada, England, Germany, Iran, Australia, Japan, South Africa—everywhere in the world. We work together via the phone or Skype and via email on all of the issues that creative folks face: survival issues, resistance and blockage, existential sadness, productivity, marketing and promoting, distraction addictions, everything.

What do I actually do? How does the coaching work? What do clients present as issues, how do I respond, and what transpires? What *really* goes on? Although I've written about creativity coaching in several books, I've never been able to show the literal work. I began to wonder if there might be a way to share with readers the actual coaching experience. Then it struck me that a way to present the complete, unvarnished experience did exist. If I limited myself to email coaching and if I asked clients beforehand if I could share our correspondence verbatim, then a reader would be able to see *everything there was to see* about how the coaching worked. It would all be there in black and white.

A lot of the questions that I am regularly asked about creativity coaching could get answered this way. What was the difference between coaching and therapy? Now a reader could see! A reader could see how in virtually every interaction one could have done therapy and how I coached instead. What do you do when a client presents a wide variety of issues? Now a reader could see! A reader could see how I focused and made choices. What do you do with a frustrated client, a sad client, a blocked client, an overwhelmed client, or an under-motivated client? Now a reader could see! It would all be there, transparent and real.

This idea intrigued me and I invited creative and performing artists who subscribe to my newsletter to embark on this adventure with me. A few hundred came forward. Many had wanted to work with me for the longest time but hadn't been able to afford my fees, so this free opportunity delighted them. All had real issues that they wanted help with. No one signed up as a lark or to be part of an experiment. All of them wanted the coaching! Now, how was I going to manage working with a few hundred clients—and for free, to boot? Had I bitten off more than I could chew? Yet the challenge excited me. I pushed my worries to the side and began.

I used the same basic set-up with each client. I invited them to answer three questions, about their history, their current challenges, and their goals for the upcoming two months. When they replied, I asked a clarifying question or two to help me better understand their situation. When they replied again I offered them my vision of what they might want to work on for the next two weeks, invited them to come to their own conclusions, and asked them to report in two weeks. When they reported after two weeks, I set them off on the next three weeks of work. And so on. That amounted to the entire set-up.

I immediately learned an interesting thing: that many of the folks who recognized that this was a golden opportunity nevertheless dropped by the wayside. Some dropped out almost immediately; others got as far as formulating what they wanted to work on for the first two weeks and then dropped out without another word or confessed that they hadn't accomplished anything and preferred not to continue. Here is how one writer put it: "Between the struggling marriage and our displaced life due to the hurricane I have not been writing. This didn't work for me. It was a great concept, though!"

In a relatively short amount of time only half the original artists remained. This is important to note, both for students of the creative process and the creative life and for coaches who want to work with creative and performing artists. Even with no fee and even with the opportunity to work with a seasoned coach, an artist is entirely likely still not to be able to make use of that opportunity, maybe because of life circumstances, maybe because of a pervasive sense of sadness and defeat, maybe because his current project is too hard, or for any number of other reasons. Naturally this doesn't auger well for folks who want to make a living from coaching! But whatever it may auger it is nevertheless the reality.

I also saw immediately that the words were piling up. How could this mass of coaching be presented in a normal-sized book? I decided that I would limit myself to presenting twenty-five clients and to presenting only the first two weeks of coaching with each client. Two weeks may seem like too small a window, as if nothing much could really happen in so short a time. But that isn't true. A great deal can happen in two weeks, including changed lives. I think you will agree as you read that two weeks proved a generous amount of time—long enough to secure a beachhead, long enough to scale a mountain, and long enough to move a creative life onto new footing.

What were the results? You will see. In some cases they will seem miraculously dramatic. In many cases you'll wonder, did anything really happen? If this were fiction, I assure you that I would have provided you with more exciting results, more breakthroughs, more glamorous clients, more gala openings and more appearances on bestseller lists, and in general a much more uplifting read. However, this is reality. It is funny that reality must almost be apologized for, just as a moviemaker is inclined to have to apologize for not providing a happy ending to his movie. However, this is exactly what toiling away in the arts looks like.

I think you will also find it interesting that while a client may say a lot I say only a little. Ninety percent of the words in this book are from clients; my responses are brief and to the point. I've learned over the decades that it is not helpful to try to address everything a client brings up, to respond in as many words as if that kind of responding guaranteed a client his money's worth, or to wait too long to start setting goals and moving forward. Coaching is not therapy and I am not investigating the past. In general I am saying two things to clients: "Given the picture you've presented, what do you want to try?" and "Given the picture you've presented, here's what I think might be valuable for you try." Saying either thing does not take many words.

What is perhaps most revealing is how much these creative and performing artists are struggling. Not one has it easy. Many are dealing with chronic health issues, relationship break-ups, overwork and overwhelm, and intense financial insecurity. There are powerful regrets, resentments, and disappointments; lingering family issues; and deep uncertainty about how to hold everything together. Many are one decent craft show or one portrait commission away from homelessness. The challenge to create or perform is on top of all of that; and it is quite regularly one challenge too many. I think that you will never again paint too rosy a picture of what real creative and performing artists are up against as they try to deal with life and with art.

I've included twenty-five of these coaching interactions in this book, exactly as they occurred. The name I've given each client is fictional; everything else is real and untouched. I've also included a short second part in which I paint a picture for coaches and prospective coaches of the essentials of coaching. I address how to start sessions, what to do when you get lost in a session, why you might want to do a lot of interrupting and a lot of inviting, what goes on between sessions, and so on. If you are a coach, a coach-in-training, or a prospective coach, a therapist or other helping professional, or a creative or performing artist thinking about hiring a coach or thinking about becoming a coach, you'll likely find this second part useful reading.

If you're a coach, you might also use this as a sort of workbook. Remember the set-up: a client introduces herself and I ask for some clarification; she clarifies and I set out the work for the next two weeks; she reports on those two weeks and I set out the work for the next three weeks. This gives you the opportunity to see what you might like to try at each of those juncture points: what clarifications you might want, how you might formulate the first two weeks of work, and how you might formulate the second three weeks of work. Of course your way may be very different from mine! I think this is a great opportunity for a coach, a coach-in-training or a prospective coach to try his or her hand at some imagined coaching.

This is in essence a very simple book, one that chronicles my email coaching work with a certain number of creating and performing artists. I think that its simplicity belies its importance. I think that you will see clearly for the first time the exact challenges that creative and performing artists face, how stuck they can get and what works to unstick them, and, maybe most impressively, how change can happen in a short amount of time. I think that these changes, when they do occur, amount to human-sized miracles.

As I've said already, please do not expect a cathartic conclusion to each story! This is not fiction and I am not manipulating the material to create fantasies and happy endings. Sometimes it will seem as if a client has gone backwards, taken a useless detour, done nothing much, or arrived at a place of greater confusion. Yet even with these unimpressive or even dispiriting results there is often a genuine silver lining: that some insights may have been gained and that some seeds may have been planted. Will these insights and seeds turn out to be enough? In many cases not, because of the hardness of the challenges involved. But for some, absolutely! Genuine progress after an inauspicious-looking beginning happens all the time!

Naturally in real life I do not work exclusively via email. I also speak to clients via phone or Skype. Still I did not have the sense that my hands were tied by virtue of having only email at my disposal. I think that my clients, too, found this to be a useful and sometimes even an exceptional experience. Maybe some day there will be a way to include the phone coaching verbatim as well, but for now I think this experiment served its purposes, both in terms of helping the clients who came forward to be coached and presenting readers with rich material.

I am excited to present this to you. Among my goals as a writer, a therapist, and a coach are to be clear and to be real. I think nothing could be clearer or more real than presenting you with the verbatim coaching, with nothing hidden, nothing paraphrased, nothing glossed over, and nothing changed. Maybe it might even become a model for sharing the actual work that other professionals like business coaches, life coaches, spiritual coaches, and even therapists do. Rather than having them tell us what they do, maybe they will show us! Wouldn't that be fascinating?

1. THE POLISH WRITER

I WORK WITH CLIENTS FROM ALL OVER THE WORLD AND THEIR ISSUES ARE REMARKABLY SIMILAR. A WRITER FACES THE SAME CHARACTERISTIC ISSUES OF WRITERS WHETHER HE OR SHE LIVES IN PITTSBURG, PANAMA, PYONGYANG ... OR POLAND.

**

Dear Eric,

I am a psychologist, a life coach and a writer. I started writing short stories the moment I was able to hold a pen a long time ago. I am pretty sure I created stories in my imagination long before that. Still at school, I won a few writing competitions. Later, at university and studying psychology, I gathered a collection of short stories and finally got them published in 2005. The book was a success. Unfortunately, the publishing company went bankrupt and I wasn't able to publish anything else with them.

In 2011 I wrote a novel for teenagers. That was a success, as well, and made me very happy to be publishing my work again (even though the publishing house also went bankrupt just recently). Soon afterwards, in 2012, I published a novel (with yet another publisher) that became a bestseller. Since then I've written yet another novel and I am currently working on trying to publish that, too.

In the meantime, between my novels, I worked full-time as a psychologist, police officer, I gained my Ph.D., taught English in a language school and did many things to simply earn money. I also became a mother and took care of my child at home until he was old enough to go to a kindergarten. It was a very intense time for me, as I decided not to go to any employer, but to set up my own business, which I did, in June this year. I set up a centre for psychology and coaching. Running it as a director and giving coaching sessions takes most of my time, even though it doesn't generate much money yet.

At this point I must tell you something important about publishing in my country. There are only a few writers who can make a living out of their work being published, and that is mainly because their work have been published and translated abroad. Apart from them, every single writer must do other things to earn money for living (it might sound like writing is a rather expensive hobby, and it's true in many cases). So even though my books were a success and even sold very well, it never gave me enough means for a living. At the moment I feel torn between trying to develop the business (that is my dream come true) and writing and trying to publish my novel.

My biggest challenges: I guess it's finding time and energy to incorporate writing into my busy work schedule, and trying to take good care of myself as well. Balancing job, writing and family life. There are days when I am very close to quitting writing, because from my past experience I learned that it doesn't bring food to the table. I feel that writing brings me loads of self-fulfillment, but I also feel so disappointed with the lack of financial success, that I try to focus my creative energy on my job at the moment (because it will have to make me prosperous at some point).

During these two months I would like to KNOW what is most important for me. I would like to CHOOSE which way to turn. And I want to feel great when I make that decision. Minimum? Making a decision without feeling torn. Maximum? Feeling fabulous with just being myself.

Best, Ursula

**

Hello, Ursula:

Since you know the situation for Polish writers and since it is unlikely (though of course not impossible) to make a lot of money from the writing, do you think that you want to continue writing if all of the following happened: you enjoyed the writing; you could make time for the writing without throwing yourself out of balance; and your work had a modest success and reached some number of readers?

That is, are the reasons to proceed (like loving writing and having readers) "enough" to outweigh the disappointments (primarily the lack of financial success)?

Best, Eric

**

Dear Eric,

I wept a little when trying to answer your questions. I was very moved by what I realized about myself. Never did I suspect anything so deep about writing and myself. I realized that I would write NO MATTER WHAT. That writing is the essential part of my being: it is the essence of my creativity and of my being in the world.

I am creative in many of my endeavors: in running psychological workshops, in managing my company, in my mothering. But these creative fields would never make up for the lack of writing stories. Even if I wasn't financially successful in publishing my work, I couldn't live without writing.

Thank you, dear Eric, for making me realize this. I feel so happy and mentally "rich" when I know that writing is my power, the engine that keeps my days going. Even when I don't have time to write - like now, fully engaged in developing my new business - I make up stories in my head. I make up stories when I drive my car, when I brush my teeth, when I cook dinner, when I swim in a pool, when I fall asleep I have incredible stories under my eyelids. Because this is who I am - a storyteller.

(Oh no, weeping again).

At the moment I am a little overwhelmed. Something beautiful happened. Let me stay with this feeling for a while.

Yours sincerely, Ursula

**

Hello, Ursula:

Good <smile>! Now let us get you writing regularly, every day. Even though you are very busy and even though you have a lot of duties and responsibilities I would like you to PLEASE WRITE EVERY DAY, first thing in the morning before your "real day" begins, if only for a few minutes. Let that be our goal, all right?

**

TWO-WEEK REPORT

Hello, Eric:

On the first day I was simply angry at having a task, that Eric gave me without asking if it's ok with me. So after reading his e-mail I immediately thought I was NOT going to do it. I thought that's not what I wanted at all. I wanted to make a decision and writing every day, when I have so many responsibilities anyway, was NOT good.

Well, what else can I say, I'm a rebellious soul. Soon after the anger receded I decided it was not a bad idea, at all. Since having a coaching opportunity with Eric is an amazing thing that is happening to me, I might as well agree to the task he gave me and simply start writing.

So I did start writing. The first morning was hard. I was staring at the blank page and nothing came to my mind. So I thought – why not start writing anything, without censoring it by my inner critic? Just write, you know, like when I was a little girl, without any agenda for writing?

And a miracle happened. The words flew out of me like birds released from cages. I couldn't stop. I had to set an alarm clock, so I don't write for too long and not get my son ready for kindergarten. The most freeing experience I've had in years.

I wrote and wrote and wrote. Some days it was half an hour, some more, some only ten minutes. But I did write down a beautiful story. Moreover, I decided not to be bounded by any ideas, and so soon I realized that the person I was writing about – the heroine of the story – was me. A touching version of me, long lost and forgotten. A girl seeking love and adventure.

After ten days I caught myself thinking about a business project I was working on. Instead of writing a story, I started writing about the project. Except that this time it was easy! It took me a long time to design that project and somehow I couldn't finish it. And what happened? Writing stories somehow unblocked my mind and I was able to finish the project in two days. For the last two days I was writing down ideas for other projects, and they too came easily.

I don't know how it happened, but letting myself write whatever came to my mind and eventually writing a good story, unblocked my creativity in another area!!! In the area of business projects. And who would have thought of that? I am leaving for a weekend in the countryside tonight. I feel wonderful. I never thought that letting myself write whatever story I like would also unleash other creative parts of me. And isn't that amazing?

Thank you, Eric

Ursula

**

Hi, Ursula:

Ah, what lovely everyday miracles there can be <smile>! Let's continue making miracles and look toward the next three weeks ...

**

As with Ursula, sometimes a client's first reaction to a strong suggestion is anger. A coach has to accept that this may happen and accept that sometimes his clients may be angry with him for making demands. If we want our clients to risk, we as coaches must also risk!—in this case, by taking the risk that an ultimately useful suggestion will be received with some initial resistance and irritation.

2. THE CONTROL ISSUE: MY FAVORITE FRIEND

ALTHOUGH WE KNOW IT AS SOON AS WE STOP TO THINK ABOUT IT, TOO OFTEN WE FORGET TO CONSIDER WHAT WE CAN ACTUALLY CONTROL IN LIFE, WHAT WE CAN ONLY INFLUENCE, AND WHAT WE CAN NEITHER CONTROL NOR INFLUENCE. WISDOM IN LARGE PART IS IN REMEMBERING THESE DISTINCTIONS! AN ARTIST CAN'T CONTROL WHETHER A COLLECTOR WILL BUY HIS WORK, WHETHER AN EDITOR WILL BUY HIS BOOK, OR WHETHER AN AUDIENCE WILL LOVE HIS CONCERTO. HE CAN, HOWEVER, EXERT ALL SORTS OF INFLUENCE. AND WHAT CAN HE ACTUALLY CONTROL? WHETHER OR NOT HE PAINTS, WRITES, OR COMPOSES! THAT HE CAN CONTROL.

**

Hello, Eric

I am an abstract painter who has been painting for about 13 years. I'm currently in five galleries and I make about 30% of my total income from art sales. The other income comes from the graphic design business that I've had for twenty years. I'd like to make 100% of my income from painting, with some supplemental income possibly coming from workshops, if needed. I sell my work at a good price point and am pleased with that. I'd like to be in more galleries but rarely have the time to search out new galleries.

I got caught in the real estate bubble in 2006. I bought a house in a place I love, with the intention of selling my other property. I was not able to sell the other property (in a place I don't really love) before the bust. Currently, I'm living in the place I love but I'm upside down in it and the other home is a rental property. I could go back to the rental and reduce my expenses dramatically. The home could be paid off in a few years and be a dramatic game changer.

I've been working both businesses (painting and graphic design) very hard for the past seven years, but I'm burnt out. IF (and that's a big "IF") I could sell this home in the place I love, I will lose about $80,000 that I need for retirement. I've been working really hard to avoid this, hoping the market would come back, but it's not in this particular area. Currently, I'd be lucky to go to the closing table and not have to write a check.

I'm emotionally exhausted from the "push" to stay ahead. My rental house doesn't make me money ... I'm at about break even. Both houses require ongoing maintenance. Obviously, this stress affects my creativity. I paint when I can which is usually on the weekends or vacation time I take to paint. Plus, I have the additional work of marketing the art through newsletters and gallery submissions, etc. Internally, I'm so happy when I see my friends push ahead and make big strides in their art careers. But it makes me sad that I'm not able to devote the time to my art to really push ahead. I feel angry that I'm caught in what feels like a trap. My brain gets caught in a victim role, which is not healthy.

I have some serious soul searching to do.

I'm just back from a group show that has been in the making for about two years. The show was a great success as far as how it was welcomed at the Art Center. (This is a notable art center that has brought in other abstract painters such as Frankenthaler and Stella, so landing the show was a feather in our cap.) The four artists involved did artist talks to a crowd of 100 patrons, with the intention of helping them understand non-representational art and where it comes from within the artist.

The Curator and Director were thrilled with the results. We made important contacts with patrons who are willing to connect us to other museums so we can take this show on the *road. All of this is really great stuff to take away from the experience. The response and feedback was better than any of us expected. And although there is still time for sales, I didn't sell one painting and it makes me question if this is a good path for me to continue based on my current situation.*

What I'd like to accomplish during these two months is a way to hang onto my creative self and to my desire to be an artist. I'm ready to leave this home that I love if I can get out of it. But I have a partner who is part of the decision. He loses about the same amount of money I do if we leave now. But we are barely hanging on and able to keep up expenses, with the majority of the maintenance expenses for the houses falling on me.

I have been financially responsible all my life but I feel I'm losing myself creatively. But to <u>not</u> be financially responsible goes against my core values. Do I put my art on hold? Do I stop creating art and do what it takes to stay here and wait it out until we can make some income off of this house? Or do I throw the money away to save my creative soul and get back to a more balanced life?

I've been juggling both and suffering from it.

Minimum goals would be to find a way to make some decisions that move me in a good direction. I need tools to help me make a good decision. I'm confused on what's important right now—to be financially responsible or find a way out to a life that is more balanced creatively.

The "WOW, that would be great" goals seem very far off to me but I am clear on them. I want a life that is less stressful and includes being in the studio every day. I want a life where I have some workshops in order to share the healing effects of creating art. I want a life where I have time to spend with other artists and to travel and visit galleries and museums. I want a life where I have time to have friends over for dinner, to visit my studio and share and critique. I want a life where I am relaxed and allow creativity to come. Right now, my thinking brain is in overdrive searching for answers and there seem to be no good answers for a way out.

I'd love your help, Eric.

Thanks, Laura

**

Hello, Laura:

Many of your core issues are not in your control, as you know. You are not in control of the real estate market or whether or not people will buy your paintings or maybe even whether or not painting can continue to interest you if you don't garner sales.

However there are some things you can control (or try to control) and there are many things that you can strive to influence. For instance, you can try to control your thoughts and think thoughts that serve you and you can try to exert some influence on sales.

But two first questions are, what exactly are the thoughts that do serve you and what influence can you exert to help with sales? So let's try to begin answering those two questions: can you list three new thoughts that might serve you (for example, "I can paint for two hours every day no matter what's going with my houses") and three things you might try to produce more sales? Let's start there, shall we?

Best, Eric

**

Hi Eric,

Thanks for your reply and input. And ah, the control issue. My favorite friend! It just helps me for you to remind me that I cannot control so many of my challenges. So thank you for that. It's amazing how much that reminder helps.

Now, onto the other suggestion you had.

I'll answer those two questions:

1. *Can you list three new thoughts that might serve you (for example, "I can paint for two hours every day no matter what's going with my houses")*

   a. *I can spend two hours a day painting or marketing/promoting my art every day.*

   b. *I can commit to meditating every day to help calm my mind and thoughts.*

   c. *I can research workshops and create a curriculum for what I'd like to teach.*

2. *And three things you might try to produce more sales? Let's start there, shall we?*

   a. *I can create a list of my top 15 galleries I would like to pursue. I can send my electronic portfolio (letter, resume, etc.) to 2-3 galleries a week, with follow-up postcards or cards mailed 3 weeks and 6 weeks later. After those 15 are sent, I can send to my secondary list of galleries.*

   b. *I can design and print a small printed brochure to mail to galleries.*

   c. *I can purchase mailing labels for art consultants that carry abstract/contemporary work and mail brochures to them.*

   I'm starting this week.

   Laura

**

Hello, Laura:

Great! The work you've outlined, then, is your work of the next two weeks, both the new right thinking (which you must persist in monitoring) and the doing.

**

Hello Eric,

Below is my report of what I accomplished, what I didn't get to and what I learned. This is such a valuable tool. I'll keep using this. Thank you again for this opportunity. I'll continue to keep my journal and look forward to hearing from you as you have time.

TO DATE:

What I accomplished:

I worked almost every day on my painting and/or market-ing of my artwork.

I sent my electronic portfolio package to six galleries. I got two positive responses. The others either weren't interested or aren't reviewing artists until Jan/Feb 2014

Sent JPGs of all available work to one gallery, along with inventory sheet since they are interested in giving me a show.

I completed my online submission to White Columns web-site, where NYC galleries review emerging artists portfolios. Awaiting news if I was juried in.

I photographed some newly completed artwork and sent them to two of my existing galleries.

Packaged and photographed and sleeved some paper piec-es for my local gallery.

Investigated FuseBox and Jing for making videos for online posting

Sent an email and image to one of my galleries who has a possible buyer who is interested in one painting and wanted the background on it.

I completed an electronic newsletter that will go out this week through Constant Contact.

I organized my studio. Moved the canvas storage bin to the storage locker and opened up a lot of space in my painting studio.

I got paid for two sold paintings.

Called about the Golden Residency in upstate NY. I am going to apply for this.

Researched Santa Fe galleries and sent out a few portfolios.

I turned down a design job that I was pursuing. In the end they kept asking me to lower my rate. Finally I said no and that was the end of that. It felt extremely good and extremely right. It was such a weight off after I did that.

Found some marketing advice that my galleries could use and sent them links.

Mentored a young artist who just graduated and is wanting to learn how to approach galleries. This was fun to do and he was very appreciative. He said I should teach workshops on this

What I did not get to:

I did not research workshops or create a curriculum

I did not design/print a small brochure

I did not purchase mailing labels for direct mail campaign to art consultants.

What I learned:

I learned that my list was a bit too aggressive for a two-week time period.

I also learned how important it is to do something every day in the studio. I really want to get to a place where I can paint every day.

I learned how much keeping a daily art journal helps me stay focused and keeps my mind from worry.

I was so busy doing my list and goals that I didn't have much time to worry about the other things I can't control.

We did have another real estate agent who came over and gave us her run down (possible sales price, etc.) which was not good news. I think the next step is to talk to an attorney and my accountant. But at least we are moving forward so we can make an educated decision.

I learned (or was reminded) that I don't have enough time in the day to do all the things I want and need. ;-)

I learned that my design business is frustrating. I'm constantly waiting on people to get me content, even though we agree upon deadlines. In the end they never hold up their end, and I always have to hold up mine. This is one reason I want to transition out of this business. I've been doing it for almost 40 years and I am certain it is time for a positive change in a new direction.

I learned that I should always say YES to great offers. That's what got me connected to you Eric and I am so grateful for your help.

I am headed back to North Carolina where my show is for an artist talk and some down time. I'll take my laptop and work on curriculum and do some research on workshops. Please let me know how to proceed.

All my best, Laura

**

Hi, Laura:

That was a wonderful amount of work. Congrats! Since you have so many things that you genuinely want to do, both with respect to the making of the art and the marketing of the art, and since there is only so much time in the day, I think that the only thing I would suggest for the coming three weeks is that you continue in the same vein but that you make a plan for maintaining a great balance among the three things that must be balanced, the art-making, the art-selling, and the rest of life. Maybe you can think through one more time what an "ideal schedule" that balances all three might look like and commit to it, remembering that doing a lot is a good thing and keeps your mind from worrying <smile>. So pencil in a lot and create a schedule that does a nice job of juggling those three balls, the art-making, the art-selling, and life.

**

Someone who has toiled in the fine art world and the commercial art world for as long as Laura has knows an awful lot about what she can control and can't control and what she can influence and can't influence. But often life rushes us along so fast and we get so caught up in unproductive obsessions that we forget to check in with ourselves and recommit to exerting influence where we can and controlling what we can. This is why we must stop periodically so as to break the grip of our unproductive thoughts, clean our mental house, and start off again on a better mental footing!

3. SIGNIFICANT ART IN 45 MINUTES A DAY

VIRTUALLY ALL OF US TEND TO SCORN SMALL INCREMENTS OF TIME AND "THROW AWAY" FIFTEEN MINUTES HERE AND FORTY-MINUTES THERE, ARGUING THAT WE ARE DOING SO MUCH ALREADY THAT THOSE WINDFALLS NEED NOT BE USED PRODUCTIVELY. WE OPT TO CHECK OUR EMAIL, SURF THE NET, PLAY A GAME, TAKE A PEEK AT OUR SOCIAL MEDIA, WATCH A FEW MINUTES OF A PROGRAM THAT WE LIKE, OR IN SOME OTHER WAY PASS THE TIME UNTIL OUR REAL WORK BEGINS AGAIN. ARTISTS WITH BUSY LIVES OFTEN FIND THAT THEY NEED TO CHANGE THEIR MINDS ABOUT SQUANDERING THESE PRECIOUS SMALL INCREMENTS OF TIME—IN PART BECAUSE SO MUCH CAN GET DONE IN JUST A FEW MINUTES!

**

Dear Eric:

I had no apparent interest or talent in art until I was thirteen, when I spontaneously began to make oil paintings. I felt a sense of joy and ease when I was making things. In my twenties I got degrees in architecture, sculpture, and family therapy. I felt like my painting and design work just happened, and assumed I would be a famous architect or artist one day, with no need for planning. I was unconcerned about financial practicalities.

In my thirties I attempted to be a businessman, did okay as an architect and in several other ventures, but never felt a sense of importance about what I was doing. Now at 58, I've spent the past 25 years working on my own, mostly designing and building furniture and objects. This work has ranged from one-of-a-kind art objects, to tasteful commissioned custom furniture. I never lived in luxury, but I had vast amounts of free time, which seemed essential to me.

I've taught a class in visual thinking at a university for the past fifteen years. The energy and time I've invested in developing projects for the course is disproportionate to the paycheck, but I have been deeply satisfied by the creative growth of my students. I feel lucky to have stumbled into a perfect teaching job, one in which I am free to experiment, and I love surprising my students (who are mostly non-art majors) by expanding their definition of what artists do. In the past four years I have morphed my classes into a hybrid format, enhancing the face-to-face time with what I think are innovative cloud-based projects allowing me more one-on-one contact with my students.

At the moment, my biggest challenge is keeping my head above water, while doing my best to care for a parent, who suddenly developed Alzheimer's in December, and for my ancient, incredible dog, who is slowly dying from a tumor. The time required is erratic, and some days I have little time to work, or take care of myself. I have benefitted from my involvement with an online meditation group, and for the first time in my life I meditate every day. We have focused on compassion and loving kindness for two months, and feeling compassion for other people has been an effective way to avoid feeling sorry for myself.

More generally, the greatest obstacle to my creativity has been my tendency to run from one passion to the next. I have excellent brainstorming abilities, and getting into 'flow' states comes easily. Staying the course, completing projects, and staying focused on what deeply matters to me, without getting distracted by what other people need, is difficult.

Three things come to mind as goals:

1. *I'd like to move back toward "Art Furniture," as opposed to making most of my income from designer/tasteful/ commissioned work. This would entail finishing a small series of pieces, photographing them, and seeing if I could place this work in 'fine craft' galleries.*

2. *I'd like to complete a book (or even something of book-let length) which records the principles and methods I've employed in my classes.*

3. *The book is in service of my bigger dream, which is to become a "Traveling Teacher," a teacher-entrepreneur who is able to work outside of learning institutions. Both in art and in teaching, my hope has been to affect a few people deeply, but now I am wondering if I could help people learn about art and creativity at a much larger scale.*

I have developed an eCourse which takes the concepts of Visual Thinking further. I am planning to offer it to a small number of former students, and if it goes well, find ways to monetize it. I have had really positive experiences in the last year learning more about meditation, and sharing, so I'm thinking maybe I might do the small one-on-one form of the eCourse, and also open up a G+ Community to any of my 900 former students, and other people who might be interested.

Hmmm: that seems a bit much for two months. So I'd say it's reasonable to 1) do sketches for new 'art' furniture ideas; 2) complete a booklet following the outline of my 15 week course; and 3) launch the G+ community and see what happens.

Matthew

**

Hi, Matthew:

The goals you articulate for yourself make good sense. But it's not so easy to tackle three disparate goals unless you create a decent schedule and create a sense of when you will be doing what. I know this is difficult given the erratic nature of your life, but I wonder if you could nonetheless try to create a daily schedule that takes these three goals into account? Would you do a little of each every day, work on one project one day and one the next, and so on? Please let me know what sort of schedule you think you might be able to create that honors these three goals and gives them a "place" in your life.

**

Hello, Eric:

Your response forced me to take a more realistic look at my present situation. I couldn't see a viable way to schedule all the things I would need to do for the three goals I mentioned, and I saw that they each had an external focus about my ambitions in teaching, publishing, showing my work, and I think what I most need right now is to support my 'inner world.'

I was sorting images yesterday, deciding what to include with my new teaching resume, and I stumbled upon a drawing I made in architecture school 30 years ago. The drawing is of a sort of magical nightclub and made me think, "I like this so much. Why didn't I continue with these sorts of drawings which combine a specific space with an emotion?"

So I've decided to focus on one thing during the next few weeks, which is to spend 45 minutes a day on two-dimensional art, with no goal other than spending the time with pens and pencils (or even an iPad), seeing what happens when I draw and paint again instead of trying to do something with a mostly external purpose.

Immediately I had ideas for several drawings. Artistic inspiration is NOT something I have a problem with. This feels like returning to what I know I'm good at, rather than focusing on finishing a book. I think I'll save the writing project for later. I can work on drawings each night. And it's very clear that this is a time when I really need to focus on self-expression, and doing something that nurtures me.

Do you think it's important to schedule my art time at a specific hour? I've had pretty good luck with my meditation practice, meditating every day this year, without trying to do it at a set time each day, so my inclination is to make sure I draw every day, without putting it in a specific time slot.

Thanks so much for your input,

Matthew

**

Hi, Matthew:

Great. That is a clear goal for the next two weeks. Let's make it happen <smile>. As to the specific hour, I do think there are certain reasons for instituting a morning creativity practice and doing our creative work "first thing" but I think the proof is in the pudding. If you are getting to your drawings every day and for enough time, then there is no reason to schedule it. If, however, you aren't getting to it every day and for enough time, then I would indeed formally schedule the time.

**

TWO-WEEK REPORT

Eric,

I was very consistent, drawing every day, and continuing to meditate, which is something I've done every day this year. But last week, I had the horrible experience of having to put my dog to sleep. He has been my 'rock' for almost 15 years. It was a remarkable time together. In people years he was 116, so I know I was incredibly fortunate. Now I'm figuring out life without him.

This has been a fortuitous time to get back to making art. I drew at 3AM several nights when I was awakened by barking, and now that I'm on my own, I spend time drawing while I'm on hikes in the beautiful park nearby. I feel like I am done with my two-week art-making warm-up, and significant themes are beginning to emerge. I was drawing plants yesterday, and then drew a water tower, which tied into a lifelong interest in archi-tecture.

I've learned that I can draw everyday, even 'in the midst' of a calamity. I've also learned that I can accomplish significant things in just 45 minutes per day.

For a long time, I have been frustrated by not being able to manifest all the ideas that are in my head. Yesterday it occurred to me that the digital drawing skills that I use in my design work can be applied to art ideas, thus allowing me to generate images much more quickly than with the hand-drawn processes I was limited to 25 years ago. A few things get better with time :)

I think for years I have used the need to make money and survive as an excuse to not make art. The reality is I never had to work 40, 50, 60 hours a week in order to get by. The past two weeks have proved I can make art for my own satisfaction, with-out it interfering with what presently pays the bills. I also know that creating art is a very therapeutic activity, which will help with whatever grieving I have ahead, and allow me to chart a course to the next stage of my life. My plan is to continue to draw everyday, and hopefully be surprised by where I'm at in two weeks.

Thanks, Matthew

**

Hi, Matthew:

That's great! (Except, of course, about the loss of your dog.). I would articulate your goals for the next three weeks as follows: to draw every day; to begin to think about and to begin to execute "themes," so that your art is less "random" and more a representation of your feelings and ideas; and to think more about how you might make use of your digital drawing skills as you move forward. The core goal is to draw every day but please also pay attention to the other two goals, to begin thinking about "themes" and to begin thinking about how your digital drawing skills might get used.

**

One of the ways that we can connect to our deepest artistic themes, themes that may be eluding us in the chaos of life, is to attend to our art so often in the day, even if just for fifteen minutes here and thirty minutes there, that our art remains close to us and has a chance to grow. Don't scorn those small increments of time that added together amount to hours, days, weeks ... even years!

4. NOT TOO OLD TO BOTHER

IS THERE EVER A TIME WHEN WE'VE GROWN TOO OLD TO CREATE? NO, NOT IF CREATING STILL SPEAKS TO US AND STILL RETAINS ITS PLACE AS A PRIME MEANING OPPORTUNITY! BUT WE MAY HAVE TO REMIND OURSELVES THAT IT'S NEVER TOO LATE AND THAT OUR REASONS FOR CREATING ARE AS POIGNANT AS EVER ...

**

Hello, Eric:

Here is my situation. I am 61 years old and live in Hawaii with my husband. We are both retired from our main careers. I was an Army nurse for 20 years, then went to law school and practiced family law for awhile. Now I write health-related articles for an online client part-time. My father is terminally ill so every few months I go back to Texas to assist with his care. When I'm home, my "schedule" is very flexible and relaxed.

I used to enjoy some art-related crafts, mostly decorating dollhouses and making shadowboxes, but I stopped all art-related activities when my kids were born (they are now 34 and 36) as I was working full-time. After I retired in 2008, I started taking creative writing classes with the Christian Writers' Guild and finished 2 levels of their courses. I pitched a novel to an agent and was asked for a full manuscript but I never followed through.

I've published the online articles, a few law-related articles in print journals, and an essay in an anthology, but can't seem to move forward with the novel at all. I think part of the problem is that I targeted the wrong market (Christian romance) but I also know that I'm afraid of rejection and my advancing age makes me wonder whether I should even bother.

When I attended a writer's retreat 2 years ago, I felt like my imagination was gone so I decided to do a little art to help me be a little more creative. I took an online watercolor class, something I'd never tried, and loved it. Since then, I've taken more watercolor classes and have also branched out into mixed media and art journaling.

I started taking a face-to-face drawing and painting class at the local senior center but wasn't sure the instructor and I were a good fit. Right now, I'm taking an online fantasy travel journaling class and will be starting another one on color theory in July. I'm considering taking a face-to-face class with another instructor this summer, or maybe in the fall. I have not sold any art or entered any contests yet but would like to do both.

My challenges are the following ones:

2. Challenges:

a. *Age: My attitude sometimes is "why bother?" I'm too old to get very far, either with the writing or the art, and I wonder if people will think I'm just pathetic if I keep trying. On the other hand, though, I have more time now than I ever did before, and it's fun, so I keep trying.*

b. *Making time: I struggle with schedules - don't like them but don't get much done without them. Right now, I claim the mornings as my own for writing and art and I do things with the dogs and my husband in the afternoons. Unfortunately, I often waste the mornings and don't get done what I wanted to do. In the summer, it's better for us to swim or walk in the AM, so I want to see if I can make myself get up and out of the house early to do that, and save the indoor projects for later.*

c. *Responsibilities: I have been flying back and forth between Texas and Hawaii for the past year. When I'm in Hawaii, I'm worried about my Dad. When I'm in Texas, I worry about my husband and the dogs. I may be starting a part-time job soon but am almost hoping that I don't get it because I don't know if I can handle it right now. However, the money would be nice.*

d. *Confidence: I like the art that I make but often wonder if I am just kidding myself about it being any good. It's not as if I've devoted the last 20 years of my life to art, so I worry that people will laugh at me if I try to sell it or enter a contest.*

e. *Mental health: I'm 60% disabled according to the VA, mostly due to PTSD and depression rather than physical issues. I see a psychiatrist every 3 months and have been able to cut way down on meds, especially since I started making art. I worry, though, that I'll sink back into a deep depression some day.*

f. *Magpie tendencies: Everything is shiny and new to me, so I have trouble focusing sometimes.*

My goals are the following ones:

3. Goals:

a. *I want to enter a certain art contest that is open to amateurs and professionals. It's a local contest that focuses on plants and animals endemic to Hawaii. I've chosen my subject but that's about it. Lack of confidence is holding me back.*

b. *I'd like to explore possibilities related to selling my art. I have a few ideas but don't know much about the market. Again, confidence is holding me back.*

c. *I would like to figure out what to do about my novel - revise it, dump it and start over, abandon it, whatever.*

d. *I want to join a plein air watercolor group that meets near my home, or at least get brave enough to paint outside by myself.*

e. I want to develop a daily art practice.

Thank you, Eleanor

**

Hi, Eleanor:

Since you know your own tendencies to be anxious, to lose interest, to have trouble finding motivation, and so on, let us keep this as simple as possible. What one project can you commit to for the next few weeks? This means making a choice, committing to it, and not second-guessing your choice or finding reasons not to do it. What project shall it be?

Best, Eric

**

Eric,

I think I will choose the most basic building block of all of my goals, which is to develop a daily art practice. I think about art every day but actually doing it hasn't been something I've made a top priority.

So, I will make art for at least 10 minutes every day, no matter what. I'll be traveling back to Hawaii next week from Texas so will have to find a way to make art in less-than-ideal circumstances, while jet-lagged, but I can do it for 10 minutes each day.

Eleanor

**

Dear Eleanor:

That sounds very sensible. Maybe 20 minutes would be lovelier <smile> but ten minutes will be excellent!

**

Okay, Eric:

Sounds good. And I will make it 20 minutes.

**

TWO-WEEK REPORT

Eric,

I'm pleased to report that I met my goal of making art for at least 20 minutes each day between July 5 and July 18. Most days, I ended up doing longer sessions but 20 minutes was all I could fit in on a few of those days.

I encountered many obstacles during those 2 weeks. July 5 was my grandson's birthday so I spent much of the day with him. For the first 4 days, I was in Texas finishing up a month of care-giving for my Dad as well as visiting with my kids, grandkids and siblings, so I was very busy.

On July 9, I flew back home to Hawaii, an 18-hour trip door-to-door, then was jet-lagged for the better part of a week. I also had some emotional issues to deal with - sadness, anxiety, depression - as well as selling a house and helping my Dad tie up loose ends.

To overcome those obstacles, I kept a journal and planned ahead in writing for the next day. As an example, the day before my flight, I decided to stick to sketching while traveling (no painting) and made sure a couple of pens and my sketchbook were in my carryon bag. On most of the days, my plan was to do the homework for an online class I was taking on art journaling, so I watched the videos ahead of time and made sure my supplies and printed materials were handy. I also decided the day before about when I would make art, if possible.

I made rules for myself, too. I love to read about art, watch videos and look at other people's work but I decided that none of that would count towards my 20 minutes, which was to be devoted to painting, sketching or doing mixed media.

Discoveries:

1. *If I make a commitment, I really can make art every day, despite a lack of privacy, jet lag, emotional issues, work, lack of motivation, etc. It just requires a little planning and thought.*

2. *I can find a place to make art even away from my studio or on the road if I want to.*

3. *If I make art every day, I don't feel guilty about procrastinating and I look forward to my session. In fact, on the last day I did two sessions.*

4. *If I make art every day, the pressure of trying to make something memorable is relieved because there is always tomorrow.*

5. *Reading about art is not making art.*

6. *I enjoyed doing pretty much the same thing every day for 2 weeks (art journaling) instead of skipping around in different projects as I usually do.*

7. *I don't like making art in public but I was able to do it.*

8. *I have more ideas if I make a habit of doing art every day.*

9. *It was easier to schedule my sessions when I was already busy, for some reason, than after I got home. When my schedule is flexible, as it is at home, I tend to put things off until "later."*

10. *I am a happier person when I make art every day, even during trying circumstances.*

This was at least my 10th attempt over the course of several years at doing something (either writing or making art) every day but I never have gotten past the first 5 or 6 days before. It feels good to know I can do it.

I think the difference this time is that I wasn't reporting in to someone else daily (which makes me resistant for some reason) but I still felt accountable. Now that I've gotten past the 2-week period, I look forward to the sessions so I plan to continue.

I'm afraid, though, that I'll skip a day in the future, which will lead to more skipped days. I have a perfectionist streak and it's hard for me to get back on track once I've slipped. I will try to go with the attitude that it's something I want to do, not something I have to do.

Thanks for this,

Eleanor

**

Hello, Eleanor:

This is great! I would like you to simply continue, following your own rules <smile> and maybe articulating for yourself what you will do if you skip a day so that that single day doesn't become more than one day!

**

When we think of artists we think of a Beethoven, a Van Gogh, a Virginia Woolf, a Picasso, a Georgia O'Keeffe. But there are millions of souls like Eleanor with creative ideas, creative instincts, and creative aspirations. Picasso may have regularly painted for forty-eight hours at a stretch but for Eleanor getting in twenty minutes a day is a real accomplishment ... and something to build on!

5. YOUR SUGGESTION TERRIFIED ME

WHAT IS A CREATIVE OR PERFORMING ARTIST HOPING TO GET FROM A CREATIVITY COACH? WHAT SHE MAY NOT BE HOPING TO GET IS THE REQUEST THAT SHE DO SOMETHING THAT TERRIFIES HER! AND YET THAT MAY BE WHAT, BETWEEN THE LINES, SHE IS REALLY ASKING FOR. IN ANY CASE, I SEE IT AS MY JOB TO HONOR A CLIENT'S DREAMS BY ANNOUNCING THAT THE THING SHE DREAMS OF DOING, WHICH CURRENTLY MAY SEEM FAR TOO SCARY TO BEGIN OR EVEN TO REALLY CONTEMPLATE, IS WHAT I WANT TO PUT SQUARELY ON THE TABLE. MAYBE SHE ISN'T READY ... BUT MAYBE SHE IS. HOW WILL WE KNOW IF WE DON'T PUT IT FRONT AND CENTER?

**

Hi Eric,

I have always loved words and theatre. Back in 1987, I graduated with honors from a degree in theatre (acting) but I found my stage fright to be crippling (wish I'd known about you then!). Ultimately, after getting married to a fellow actor (we met at theatre school) and having 2 children, I ended up teaching voice and working as a director with a small theatre company, which I loved.

The company was founded on "Christian principles" which at the time were very meaningful to me. We did good work and my colleagues were generally sincere, collaborative, and talented. It was exhilarating to be in such a creative atmosphere. The job also involved creating a resource center and teaching workshops and organizing conferences. It was an "umbrella job", incorporating so many things I loved doing: directing, writing, reading, teaching, organizing resource libraries and conferences, empowering new artists, all within a spiritually-sensitive context. Other than the fact that there was next to no money, it was my "perfect job."

I had also started writing freelance articles, something I'd done on and off since I was a teenager. I used to joke that I, who suffered so badly from stage fright, had undertaken a theatre degree rather than face the terrors of writing! Moving forward in this direction was largely due to meeting working writers through my theatre work. Then my marriage ended and I couldn't juggle supporting my two young children with the erratic hours and inadequate pay of theatre work, so I started working at a library.

I wrote freelance (food, health, parenting, spirituality) and went back part-time to writing school. I wrote a novel and some picture books of my own. While I received positive feedback from teachers, classmates, and even 'placed' in a couple of contests (children's books), I did not manage to publish anything other than the magazine articles. Promoting my own work has always been very difficult.

I had grown very uncomfortable with my new identity: in the church I had been attending (I left) and my sense of who I was (divorce was not ever on my to-do list) and as a writer (I felt too exposed). Around this time, I began a new relationship. After five years, without formally marrying, we set up house in a new part of town and I essentially stopped writing. We were busy learning how to "be" in our new family dynamic, a regular writing gig had ended, and I decided I was sick of my own voice.

In the meantime, I began my training as a counselor and then started a business as a professional organizer. I enjoy the work but in spite of the many balls in the air, still feel that I am avoiding the "real work." And so, I feel bad, guilty, depressed, etc. way too much of the time. I am acutely aware that the years are passing (I'm 49) and that I have a tendency to burn out with "ide-

aphoria" and disperse my energy into too many projects. While this has made me empathic towards my chronically disorganized clients, I too can feel "flaky" and "unfocused" and unsuccessful much of the time (in spite of being organized!) It probably comes as no surprise that I've struggled with depression: during my first marriage, after the birth of my second child, and in truth, probably on and off, since I was about twelve.

As to challenges: I work a lot. I currently work part-time at the library still and then with a few private clients in my organizing business. In my current business model, there is a great deal (probably too much) support work in this, and I find myself putting in lots of unpaid hours. I also have a mother-in-law with age-related health issues that takes up a fair amount of time and energy. She and her son/my partner have a complicated relationship and a lot of her care falls on me. I'm working on boundaries (with both of them!) And I feel a tremendous pressure to make up for lost time and to improve my financial state. "Indulging" in creative projects feels, well, indulgent. Lastly, I am afraid ... of something.

Afraid to commit the time? Afraid of being seen? Of not offering something worthwhile? Of adding more "noise" to an already crowded world? Of having wasted so much time? Of not being worthy? Of harboring a lifelong dream that perhaps is no longer relevant? Of having grown "out of shape" as a writer? Of it being too late? Of being boring? Hmmm. Having said that, I'm not sure I care so much just why I have such anxiety, as I do to find a way past it. I know I want to write again. I can feel the impulse but still I avoid it, except my journal, articles for work, emails for clients, etc. And everyday I don't do it, I feel another twist inside -- the anxiety has won again -- and this ultimately leads to all kinds of existential despair!

My minimum goals would be to:

1. Write creatively 3 times per week, one hour per session. I'm less concerned with the final product than I am with breaking through the impasse!

2. *Spend an additional 1-2 hours per week to review and revise some existing picture book manuscripts and find possible markets for them*

3. *Learn how to use Scrivener (though perhaps that's the kind of "around the edges" work I excel at when I am avoiding the scarier stuff)*

4. *Complete an article that I've recently started research-ing (I think I will end up doing this regardless as it re-lates to work)*

5. *To re-launch my blog on my business website and pub-lish weekly*

6. *To write and make a 5-minute movie...*

There are others, but I'd be happy with goal #1 :)

My "WOW" goal during the next two months would be to complete a Newberry Award-winning novel from which an Acad-emy Award-winning film is made. :). My also "wow" goal would be to complete a first draft of that novel.

That's all for now!

Best, Marisa

**

Hello, Marisa:

Enough of these past small projects <smile>! Let's get that novel written and published. Can you describe it to me in two or three sentences: who is the audience and what is it about?

Secondly, please pick some things that you will stop doing or do much less of, like extra work with clients and mother-in-law things. Please name the things you will quit or do less of and HOW you will quit them: that is, what do you need to say and to whom do you need to say it?

Best, Eric

**

Hi Eric,

Wow. I expected you to ask me to do something like 'commit to writing 3 times a week,' etc. I was terrified by your suggestion to get this novel written! Which meant all kinds of thoughts/emotions erupted as did all kinds of complicated developments in the other demands on my schedule. ;)

Here goes...

1. The Novel

I am fascinated by something I read in a non-fiction work about the history of women and cookbooks. The authors suggest that in the margins of recipe books, women "wrote themselves into being." This novel would be a young adult novel but would also potentially crossover to appeal to women of all ages.

12-year old, Ginny is sent to spend the summer with her grandmother while her mother juggles a new job, childcare, and eldercare, not to mention her own complicated relationship with her mother. Ginny is angry and resents being "babysat"; so does Grandmother. Tasked with doing some cooking, Ginny finds an old, annotated recipe book. Each recipe she makes ultimately serves to reveal chapters of the history and inter-related stories of these women.

2. The Not-doings

This is particularly hard...

1. *I will tell my mother-in-law I can see her regularly, but schedule it for every second or even fourth week.*

2. *I will honor my partner's right to have or not have a relationship with his mother, but I will also honor my own boundaries and levels of responsibility.*

3. *I will assist her in finding appropriate services and resources, but I do not need to be the service and resource.*

4. *I will not reply immediately to emails and phone calls but allow myself to pause and respond rather than react. I will designate time for responding rather than "getting it out of the way" which usually takes the place of writing time, etc.*

5. *I will stop putting 100% into things I don't want and instead do what matters first (i.e. writing, sleeping, exercising, moving my business into new directions)*

6. *I will continue to provide great follow-up notes for clients but recognize they needn't be Pulitzer-prize essays. (My writing has other outlets!)*

7. *I will be more conscious of the impostor-syndrome thoughts/feelings of inadequacy that often spur my tendency to overcompensate clients. I will try to be aware of when I am offering from generosity rather than anxiety.*

Thanks very much,

Marisa

**

Hi, Marisa:

Okay, that is excellent! Now you need to pay daily attention to the novel, spending real time each day on it, and daily attention to not doing the things you are now not doing! Let's consider that the work of the next two weeks.

**

TWO-WEEK REPORT

Hi Eric,

Eric Maisel

Here are my 2 weeks so far.

Week One

I got off to a slow start because of previous commitments but began in earnest (well, began might be an overstatement as you'll see!) on the 15th.

Mon, July 15: Avoided most of the day, made a few notes, created a scheduled.

Tues, July 16: Really succeeded in avoiding. Had scheduled writing from 7-9. Finally took a stab t 9:30. Some very rough character sketches, scene outline ... felt very panicky. All day have been thinking about previous experience with writing a novel. It was during a writing course and the structure was to "write five pages for next class" (creating a unique form of novels!) Attempting to organize "scenes " (writing cups?) this time. Don't know if good idea or bad. Feeling too "outside." Maybe should just write freehand for a bit rather than on computer?

Wed, July 17: Plan: write 1 scene in 1 hour. 5 pages?!! Time limit or word limit? Reality: Super-tired. Suspect it's real fatigue, also suspect it's fear (wanted to go to bed right after dinner!) Feel molasses-y. Afraid that I am more comfortable writing about writing, than I am writing. This project is more complicated than anything I've attempted before. I am not sure how to proceed. Every day I think about it more. I feel anxious all the time.

Thurs, July 18: So not a lot of actual writing today but I did do yoga, and meditated and tapped and felt much better. Ideas keep coming. Struggling between structure and exploration. Leaning towards former.

I wanted to try creating an outline this time as I had the sense it would be more helpful once I'm further along due to the layered timelines of this novel BUT am missing the sense of getting caught up in the "dream" while writing (outlines don't do it for me). Got panicky. Started random scenes. They fizzled.

48

Realized two things: 1. My "scenes" weren't really going anywhere as I needed some kind of structure to organize around... so lots of catch-22/chicken & egg stuff going on. Part resistance, I know, but also partly reality given the elements I was striving for. 2. My anxiety was (is!) REALLY high and I got/get overwhelmed very easily

Decided to just give it some "attention" every day and show up.

Fri, July 19: Nothing today. Decided to track down a copy of Eat My Words (book that inspired idea) I've never read the actual book and thought seeing it again might inspire some activity.

Saturday: Nothing today. Decided timing was bad, debated quitting/dropping out, yadda yadda.

Sunday: Started reading Eat My Words, taking notes. Got very excited. Ideas are beginning to bubble!!!

Week Two

Monday: Am feeling the way I used to about researching non-fiction articles: excited by the ideas and connections that are forming.

Tuesday: Am ok that I am doing research. Does not (yet) feel like avoidance but a way in. Strong ideas for structure coming out of my notes.

Wednesday: Finished reading book. Feel like I need some historical research for each of the chapter periods BUT think I can start without (or do concurrently)

What I know so far

1. *Paying attention to self-care like yoga and (especially) meditation is not a form of avoidance but a useful way to manage my anxiety and a way into the writing (I noticed a shift after July 18)*

2. *Research is not inherently a form of avoidance and for me in this particular case feels like a way in. I can use it to get excited about what I am doing (I have enough experience with writing non-fiction and doing research that I believe I am being honest here.)*

3. *I have decided that set times are useful but they need to have actual tasks assigned to them. At this point, I am still too anxious and will easily spend two hours not doing anything. To that end, I need to set some concrete goals.*

4. *Even if I don't physically write on a particular day, I can enjoy thinking about the story and "falling" into scenes. This sense of pleasure in imagining makes it more appealing and less scary to return to the writing.*

5. *You used a phrase: "Pay daily attention" to the novel and while I know you also said "spend real time" it is the first part that has been the most helpful the past two weeks. In my most anxious moments, I have reminded myself to simply "pay attention." That's been helpful in terms of allowing both the novel and the process to begin to open and to feel pleasurable. (Like many people, I'm inclined to a fair amount of self-loathing and punitive inner voices -- neither of which have been very helpful!)*

So all of this and I have not "written" anything of substance but I do feel that this is now possible in this next section of time.

Thanks, Eric. I look forward to hearing from you again.

Best, Marisa

**

Hello, Marisa:

Please actually write the novel <smile>. If that means sitting in complete anguish and misery for three straight hours and refusing to go anywhere and getting exhausted and ranting at the process and hating life and me, so be it, but you must learn to sit there and write the novel—unless, of course, it is really too soon for that and you have no idea what you are writing about and need to incubate it more.

I hope that you will say to yourself that you do not need to incubate it more but rather need to face the blank page, with all its terrible blankness. But you get to decide how to spend the next three weeks, doing things "that serve the writing" or sitting there in agony and writing. I of course vote for the latter <smile>!

**

Is Marisa ready to write her novel? Aren't you curious to read her next three-week report? What's your hunch? Will she have taken up the challenge and begun writing her novel, will she have worked "around" it, or will she have fled the encounter altogether? If you want to be a creativity coach one day, think about the following question: what might you do next in each of those three cases, including the "happy" case of her actually having started?

6. GROUND ZERO AGAIN

Some novels are clear to their author from the beginning. Most are not. Many amount to a rollercoaster ride over a several year period where the author takes five steps forward and nine steps back, returning again and again to "ground zero": the very beginning. Would any author embark on this rollercoaster ride if he knew what was coming? Yes, probably ...

**

Hello, Eric

I'm a graphic designer with a reputation for building identities and branding positions for companies (mainly hi-tech nowadays, but from all walks of business). When this is on, I earn well. The only reason it isn't always 'on' is that I withdrew from it about four years ago (after twenty-five years of 100% dedication), went walkabout in France and then parts of England. I was re-evaluating what I do.

In fact I started a novel, my main new project direction. I set my standards high (the top), so this novel has been through several iterations (is probably the equivalent of having written several novels). I sent a preliminary three chapters to a publisher, who wrote back saying they liked it. It stunned me. I couldn't write for three months, and when I started again I still didn't feel good enough. It's only recently that my confidence levels are getting near to what they had always been in graphic design.

The challenge now is to finish the damn novel. I have a hot lead for an agent. I'm about two weeks away from perfecting (whatever that is) my first fifty pages. The rest of the manuscript is there but in pieces -- the order not established, tenses and points of view needing re-ordering. I tell myself that once the first fifty pages are aligned 'correctly' the rest will flow. But the work in getting these fifty pages 'right' has staggered me. It's really a new book but a lot of the old writing is (I consider) too good to waste.

I believe the biggest challenge when writing is:

A. Remove ego

B. Maintain a consistent viewpoint and avoid unnecessary re-writing

C. Edit away my more florid descriptions and too high reaching sentences. I'm inclined towards poetry. When I'm in that frame of mind I become super-creative but rather not of this world. My other editing self is more Germanic. Sometimes there's a lack of clarity as to who is writing. I have no current strategy for dealing with this.

D. Try not to worry about money or the hideous amount of time this novel has already consumed.

E. It's a true story based on my family history and I have to avoid worrying about my family's eventual opinion once this is published. I'm ignoring this aspect for the most part, but it nags me occasionally.

My aims: to get a manageable manuscript complete, circa 100,000 words minimum. Quantity does not appear to be the issue, but linking sections and weaving the story lines is. I'd also like a powerful agent backing me -- I don't just want an agent, I want the best. That scares me, and hence my delays in approaching people. I figure I get one chance and I want to send them something irresistible. It would be wonderful to see this as a career change, providing I might earn enough to get by. I'm not writing for that reason, but such thoughts do accompany me.

Thank you, Eric.

Best regards, Jack

**

Hi, Jack:

Can you clarify a little? An editor liked the first three chapters but you didn't like them? I think that I don't quite understand how that played itself out<smile>.

Can you also clarify the following? You say that that you want a top agent and you also say that you want only a manageable manuscript, which sounds like you mean that the book wouldn't "really be all that good" at that point? Can you tell me if you want to "just finish the damn thing," if you want to work on it until it is good (however long that takes), or something else? I'm feeling not too clear on your actual goals and ambitions for the upcoming weeks and months.

Best, Eric

**

Hi, Eric:

Maybe I've not been clear, because on this one area of my life I do seem to be confusing myself. Every time I sit down and write or edit I feel like I'm constantly interrupting myself. I'm doing more loops than straight lines.

So here's the jumble: I want it to be first class. I want it to still be in print five hundred years from now. I'll also do whatever it takes to finish the damn thing. And I will send it in even if it's imperfect, as long as I can find an agent who cares enough to work with me.

How I got here:

Instead of writing to agents I got on a plane and went the Frankfurt Book Festival. I cruised the exhibition stands thinking to myself who did I like the look of, and then honed in on one publisher (a matter of colors and taste and the length of their floor space). I got talking to a North American rights manager, soft-

ened her up, got the name of whom to contact in London (who turned out to be the top editor). So I sent my three chapters to them, breaking all the rules of the trade by applying directly and without an agent representing me. She evidently passed it down to an assistant.

I only had these three chapters and, being new to novel writing, I was struggling to complete a full manuscript. I was out of my depth. Taking the publisher's advice I contacted three agents. One liked it but said he'd recently decided to only deal with celeb authors. Another two agents never replied. I felt lost and rather isolated. I called up the publisher to discuss, but was told that they'd never heard of the person who wrote me the letter. In other words, you are a nobody and go way.

I just thought: sod it. I'll finish the manuscript and then I'll return to finding an agent. Two years and much work later I sent a slightly revised version to an established author, who laid into it a bit, pointing out point-of-view drift (OMG, yes, that was true) and suggesting it should be in first-person rather than third - that third person is harder to get accepted by agents and editors nowadays. So I went to India and spend 40 solid days drafting out a first person manuscript (I choose 3 POVs). At this time it was looking like two books, and that this manuscript would be book 1. But I'd climbed the mountain: I had a rough MS.

Before sending it to an agent someone recommended I discuss this with a certain TV script editor, who really looked at my work seriously. Her advice was it should definitely go third-person. She also convinced me that this was one book and not two and that as strong as some of the characters were in my first draft they didn't all earn their keep in the story, that I should know my story better, etc.

Her advice was the most thorough and helpful I've ever received, so I wrote a test piece and bounced it off her. It meant the possibility of a complete rewrite, but I thought, if that's what it takes, I'll do it. Anyway, she loved the new opening chapter; it im-

pressed her greatly. So back to ground zero again. I reconstructed a suitable three chapters, which is where I am now. I'm in the process of checking it through before I send it off to the agent I have in mind or other agents.

Mostly I feel confident that I can now be my own judge of things, and I have loads of sections and earlier drafts to adapt, so how can I fail, etc. At other times I'm frustrated at how long it takes and how errors and sentences that don't work still litter my pages. I'm reading sections out loud now more than before, which helps. I don't like hearing myself read, but figure I must do this or fail.

My aims: to feel happy enough with the first three chapters to send them to an agent. Next, feel confident I can rough out the manuscript fairly pronto, so it's there if asked. Next, bunker down for rejection and let it bounce off me. Next, just finish it, whatever. Next, find life after the book. It's been a long haul flight. I'm in danger of thrombosis.

Kind regards, Jack

**

Hello, Jack:

That does help. I fear you have the cart before the horse. Forget about "perfecting those three chapters." Write a good book first, good all the way through, as good as you can make it at this moment. Please write the book! No "roughing out the book pronto"—that isn't the right plan. It would be a shame to sell an agent on the first three chapters and then do some rush job on the book. Let's bite the bullet and get the novel written! If you agree, and I hope you do, then that's your job for the next two weeks: working daily on getting the book "really" written.

**

TWO-WEEK REPORT

Hello, Eric

Structure has been the main issue: point-of-view and the sequence of time. It surprised me to find myself revisiting these fundamentals and having to establish a revised framework. Part of the shock was losing the POV of who I thought was a main character. This was 35,000 words of writing that pleased me, but which I now have no use for. I painfully put this to one side. The central line of the story has become clearer to me, so that previous writing no longer earns its place.

I'm doing what the book demands and I'm no longer forcing my own will upon the writing. I took the two-week period of self-coaching seriously: I asked myself questions and gave myself the answers. I realize that to write is to take responsibility for my writing. I believe my main impediment in successfully writing this project is my ego — ego in terms of fear, not being good enough, trying to defend my reputation to myself as well as others, fear of failure, fear of not being able to complete, fear of not being productive enough -- and so on.

So two weeks and where am I with all this? Aware of the great distance to go (again), that a lot of my previous writing was merely preparation. I set off before I knew enough about structure and its importance, even when (in my hurry) I thought I had it sorted, I hadn't thought things through enough even when I thought I had (I guess I didn't know enough what the core of the story was). It's humbling to admit how long that process took. Knowing what I know now I could have saved myself about three years. I need to listen more to what the story wants to be and not what I want it to be.

**

Hello, Jack:

What a ride! I dearly hope you are on track now <smile>.

Let us continue in the same vein for the next three weeks, "writing a good book all the way through"!

**

Doesn't this journey give you a headache or a stomachache? Don't you wonder if Jack is finally on track or still at sea? Don't you also wonder if perhaps he has tossed many great bits, tossing them because on the day he read them they suddenly seemed off? This is the maddening, poignant journey that we so wish might prove easier and might at least come with a guarantee of a good outcome! But of course it can't and it doesn't ...

7. THE VILLAGE JAZZ SINGER

CREATIVE AND PERFORMING ARTISTS LIVE AND WORK IN VILLAG-
ES ALL OVER THE WORLD. IN THE BOLIVIAN COUNTRYSIDE, THE
UGANDAN COUNTRYSIDE OR, AS IN THIS CASE, THE DUTCH COUN-
TRYSIDE, MEN AND WOMEN PRACTICE THEIR INSTRUMENTS, PRIME
THEIR CANVASES, AND PEN THEIR POEMS. ARE THEIR DREAMS ANY
LESS SHINY BECAUSE OF THEIR RUSTIC SURROUNDINGS? NOT RE-
ALLY: YOU DON'T HAVE TO LIVE IN NEW YORK CITY TO REVERE AND
DREAM OF BECOMING BILLIE HOLIDAY.

**

Hi Eric,

I sing Jazz and Blues, and started studying the piano 3 years ago. I am 61 years now and started taking singing lessons about 15 years ago. Before that I used to sing along with records since I was about 19 years old when I started to live on my own.

I really wanted to make music with other musicians but I was shy about my performance and my singing. So for many years I just sang along with records, listened to beautiful singers and was feeling envious and helpless. Then, around 1982, I started playing the tenor saxophone, Jazz. I felt more secure with something between the audience and me.

I worked hard as an amateur, did a lot of workshops and played in an amateur brass band. But it didn't feel good. I stopped playing sax, and felt disappointed. Because what I deep down wanted was to sing. When I moved from Amsterdam to a more rural area in Holland, I met a very nice person, and she was a singing teacher. With her I started taking singing lessons. Later, there were other teachers, some good and some not so good.

But I kept feeling very insecure and scared to perform and sing and seize the moment. I was scared of competition, of compliments, of judgments, and needed a lot of affirmations from my teachers and co-musicians in the workshops I followed and sessions I participated in. Looking back I know now that I could not place these feelings then as being scared and insecure. I was then waiting and hoping for someone to recognize my talent and to rescue me and manage me (and protect me).

I was not committed to my own talent. I was afraid to stand out, to show myself, to stand upright, with eyes open, in the spotlight. And the teachers did not address this side of me. So I could not really talk about these issues. Only in the past few years, also with help of your books and your coaching training, I have learned to put it in perspective. To look at the whole process, the bigger picture, of me as a creative person and all the "issues" that that brings with it, the responsibility you have to yourself, the commitment it needs to let you be the best you that you can be.

My biggest challenge right now is to internally change myself more, to be committed to myself as a singer, every day, and respect myself, every day. Some people may call it "belief in yourself" but I'd rather call it self-respect. I also have to learn to endure and to allow myself to be my very best. Not the very best I think others expect from me but the very best I can be to myself. Not to fall apart when someone compliments me, shares the moment with me. Not to fall apart when someone gives a toxic comment, a snide remark or makes fun of me. Not to fall in the trap of the madness of the day.

I need to become my own person. And to understand myself as a creative person, to understand what I daily need to feed my creative person. That will need a change in my thinking, because my whole life I have been thinking I need the love of others to become me. I think now that first I need the love of me to become me. I am allowed to love myself first.

My minimum goal is to have a daily routine to affirm my self-respect, my talent as a singer and to allow myself to be as *good as I can be as a singer/musician. To have the freedom to do the songs I want to sing, in my own way, in my own tempo, in my own voice. My absolute, WOW goal is to choose the songs and do them in my own way. Then to put myself out there, in the music market, and organize gigs for myself. And keep doing it. Keep doing it, keep being challenged by this mean old world and still be standing.*

All the best, Linnea

**

Hi, Linnea:

I suspect that your "wow" goal has to be your minimum goal, because the way to "earn" your self-respect is to actually do the things that you name as elements of your "wow" goal. Don't you think? That would mean to have the freedom you name but to also "manifest" that freedom by choosing songs to sing, practicing them, and finding places to sing them. I wonder if you agree that your "minimum goals" and your "wow goals" need to go hand-in-hand and become your actual goals for the coming period?

Best, Eric

**

Hi Eric,

Thank you very much for your response and suggestion. It is a bit scary to put my 'wow' goal in the minimum goal. I preferred a bit of leeway for this big jump, but you are right. I can earn my self-respect and manifest my freedom by making this my actual goal for the coming period.

Thank you for your help.

Linnea

**

Hi, Linnea:

Okay, then. You have some very clear goals for the next two weeks. Attend to them in a daily way <smile>!

**

TWO-WEEK REPORT

Monday, 8 July

I made a daily to-do list to start working with my goals.

A DAILY ROUTINE

Chose one song every day to work on

Study the chords, the melody, and the position of the fingers

Study playing while singing the song

Make a practice recording and then listen to the recording

Find one address to play a gig, and add that to the database you made (in Belgium, the Netherlands, and Germany)

Tuesday, 9 July

I started the daily routine.

I chose 'Come Rain or Come Shine'. I worked on it like I suggested in the daily routine.

Then I listened to my recording. My first reaction was that I felt disappointed in what I heard. I wanted to hear a combo playing, with Billie Holiday singing (well, it would also be great if there would be Ella Fitzgerald singing...). And I didn't hear that. That was a big disappointment. To recognize this feeling of failure, to hear my inner voice speaking to myself, was a big eye opener. How could I ever reach that or compete with that in mind?

So, I took a deep breath. And listened again. And again. And accepted that what I heard was me. Was okay. Could not be different. Was not different. Was me. Now.

Then I started to work on it. What did I like in what I heard? What did I like in the way I played the keyboard? Did I need to hear more power chords? Were the little notes placed in a way that I felt was in the right moment? What "worked" and what would I change to make it better within this version of me doing "Come Rain or Come Shine"? Could the singing maybe be a bit brighter? Was the tempo a little slow or should I try it a bit faster????

Wednesday, 10 July

I have to adjust my daily routine-list. I need to work on one song for two days. I need the time to brew on what I heard, how I played it. And I need the time to try out the changes I want to make.

What an eye-opener it was to accept my playing and singing as a solo musician.

Monday, 15 July

I am working on my second song. There are a few things on my mind:

I think not often enough clear thoughts. I used to think more or less obsessive thoughts (about feelings, or social networking things). I used to worry a lot also. And also have just under the surface of my consciousness a lot of noise, a lot of foggy, random thoughts, fragments of images, memories, all passing fast. When I realized this, I wanted to change it. I decided I needed to use my brain more. Since I am doing that, I experience more structure in my day as well as more direction.

I decided to <u>stop</u> taking everything I see, meet, or hear personally. This is a big, big issue for me because I have done just that my whole long life. I realize now that taking things personal-

ly takes me from my path and takes me further away from where I want to be. It only brings me into the chaos and madness of other people's worlds where, most of the time, I don't want to live.

I used to think that, because I can pluck music-notes right out of the air, every one could do that. Well, that is not so. To realize that made me realize I have a gift. A gift I should nurture and treat respectfully (even when all the other musicians around me in the jam-session don't want to treat me respectfully). Realizing, the plucking, to me, is only beautiful when I can do it in my way, my tempo, my consciousness. It is not beautiful when I let myself be bullied to another tempo, another key, another feeling of the song.

Wednesday 17 July

I've decided to find myself a living role model for my singing. Billie Holiday and Ella Fitzgerald have been in my life for years, as singers, as musicians, as daily life personalities and as performers on stage. They were a great, big, infinite well of inspiration. I love them with all my heart. I owe them so very much.

But the world has changed. The music industry has changed, performing and audiences have changed. I need a modern singer I can relate to. So I picked Gretchen Parlato. I am very much in awe with how she sings. Technically how she shapes her words and her sound. And also her personality on stage. She sings with her eyes closed, very concentrated and surrendering to her music. At the same time she is in touch with her audience, emotionally available in the moment. No Hollywood diva-extravaganza. She helps me to get stronger in my podium moments. It's not that I want to become like her, but I like to learn from her podium presence. In a way she teaches me to take myself seriously as a singer, not an entertainer.

Thursday, 18 July

I work part time as a cleaner in people's houses. While I work I sing, with or without my little MP3 player. During the three- or four-hour shift there is a period of time that I can sing *with mental freedom. No self-censorship, just clear concentration and solid presence. Now I teach myself to remember that state of mind in other moments. It also has to do with moving, being in motion. And a certain detachment to my singing is needed.*

For the past few years I have lived in a very small village. I have done my very best to connect to people, find some common ground. But I stand out in this society like a sore thumb. I have suffered a long time the gossip, been ignored and excluded. Been insulted and made fun of behind my back, been nicknamed a scornful name half the village tell each other behind my back. Whenever people my age see me they say to each other: ah that's ... and they smile wearily so as to make the point to me, they think what a silly person I must be. Younger people start giggling and comment among themselves in a negative way about the way I look. The hostility hangs in the air.

It took me a long, long time to help myself to deal with all this. I read books that help me to acknowledge my need for my mental freedom. Not to lean on others to give it to me, but to live it myself. The remembering is also needed to affirm myself as a creative person. Ah yes, I am a singer. It's an affirmation, a positive affirmation of my creative person. And it helps me to feel good about myself. Feel proud of myself. It helps me to stay standing upright in this society. The remembering also helps me to keep focused on my goal, it helps me to feel at home somewhere, it helps me to be me.

Friday, 19 July

Today I have opened up to a friend, and have written her about my hard times in this small village. And I feel very unburdened. I don't feel guilty anymore about the way I live my life. It is filled with music, and not so many people. I choose for music, I commit myself to my goals. And I realize I can't have it all.

Monday, 22 July

The last day of this journal. Some evaluation: the daily to-

do list is not done daily. Not every day I was motivated enough to really do the work. I dabbled a lot, to get rid of some anxiety, but I was not internally convinced about my own possibilities. I experience the clash with the outside world in a negative, judgmental way. I feel/hear/see reactions of others about my age, about my looks, about my posture, about the way I drive my car etc. etc.

Well, this helpless feeling went on for some days. Even though, just a few days ago I decided to ignore all those negative influences from the outside world. I mean I made an adult, conscious decision and told myself to ignore all that hostility. I find it very difficult to ignore all that and shield myself from it. I can't seem to stand my ground. Or help myself to reach my goal.

**

Hello, Linnea:

That was such beautiful, important work—perhaps especially at the beginning <smile>. It sounds like you really bit into the task those first few days and then something—doubts, resentments, disappointments, fatigue, anxiety, something—started to get in the way again.

I think you did a lot of wonderful work but I also hope that for the next three weeks you can do that real, important work every single day, even if you feel resistance or "aren't in the mood" or sink a little. Please try to keep with this important work, to get where you want to with the songs, to reach out and make contacts, and to live well even in your too-small village.

Please recommit and work as you did those first few days, facing everything: your doubts, your voice, your situation, everything!

**

Some artists live in New York lofts and start their days at Starbucks. Other artists live in small European villages and start their days cleaning other people's houses. Each may have the same dream, the same soul, and the same aspirations. But how small, confining and unhelpful that small village may become! Like time, place is a reality in a creative person's life. When you coach creative and performing artists it is good to know where they live! The reality of place really does matter.

8. THE SAME ATTENTION

VERY OFTEN A CREATIVE PERSON IS ALSO A PERSON WHO LOVES TO HELP OTHERS, SERVE OTHERS, AND HEAL OTHERS. ALSO VERY OFTEN, THAT CREATIVE PERSON DOES A BETTER JOB OF HELPING, SERVING AND HEALING OTHERS THAN SHE DOES MONITORING HER OWN CREATIVE LIFE AND MANIFESTING HER OWN CREATIVE POTENTIAL. THEN THE COACHING IS ABOUT INVITING HER TO PAY THE SAME ATTENTION TO HER OWN CREATIVE LIFE AS SHE LAVISHES ON OTHERS!

**

Hello, Eric

I started writing and publishing in 1990 mostly in literary journals. During that time I published a chapbook and started the framework for a novel with a mentor through the Manitoba Writer's Guild. I was also drawing, mostly giving the work away. It was easy for me to get published and I had the support of the writing community.

My interests then branched out to include healing, whole foods cooking, and shamanism. I trained for five years in Hawaiian Huna Kane, Reiki, NLP, etc. In the past few years I started writing creative non-fiction, and again getting the work published. So, there have been many stops and starts, which in itself isn't bad, and all these other things are things I wanted to do.

What is difficult is that when I don't create, I don't feel fully alive. I feel like there is always something that I am NOT doing and it takes away enjoyment from those other things in life that are pleasurable. I work in publishing full-time, where I get to be creative in a lot of ways, but unless I am creating and producing something that is meaningful to me, I feel incomplete. I have also taught writing workshops and have recently developed a work-shop for writing a book in a day, etc. I help others have creative breakthroughs and I'd like to give myself that same attention.

I've been working on a Boreal Trilogy for over a year (part 1 is published), am rewriting a children's book (on the back burn-er), planning another children's story, drawing boreal mermaids and my cat (cartoonish style drawings for the cat), but I'm not finishing any of them. When I went to a book launch last week I realized that the difference between us is that she takes her cre-ative life seriously, and I don't. That's what I'd like to change. I did a session of EMDR with a friend last week which was interest-ing because since then I've felt less like helping everyone else and more like creating space for me to create, which is why I leapt at responding to your email so quickly.

My biggest challenges right now: Feeling like what I may have to add to the huge pile of what is being done is too insig-nificant or unimportant and having a limited amount of time to work on things. I think the procrastination about my work not mattering is more of a challenge than creating the time. I'm not a person with overall low self-esteem, but this is the area where I get stuck.

My minimum goal for the next two months would be to get the Boreal Trilogy finished. A wow goal would be to write the story of Ernie and Dash, a children's book on leadership in the Antarctic based somewhat on Ernest Shackleton's journey.

Best, Annette

**

Hello, Annette:

You say that you worry about the work mattering. What is the Boreal Trilogy, who is its audience, does it matter to you, and do you think it might matter to others? I'm curious to hear what you mean by writing mattering or not mattering, since that seems to be a key in your own mind as to why (or why not) to proceed.

Best, Eric

**

Hi Eric,

For three years I worked on a project called Boreality, a collaboration between artists, the boreal forest (four trips into the boreal) and the people that live there. This resulted in a concert with the Manitoba Chamber Orchestra (creating sacred music out of the landscape instead of text), and a special issue of Prairie Fire on boreal writing.

While I was working on this project, I was inspired to write (only somewhat fictionalized) about the three times I'd lived in a boreal community (age 8, 16 and 20). Each part of the Boreal Trilogy explores a connection with the landscape (rocks/trees, water/boreal mermaids and the land/nurturance). Part 1 was published in the Boreal issue.

I received some good feedback, and yes, I think the story matters. I think it's creating overall that doesn't matter. I work fulltime, have other commitments, etc., and I leave my creative work to the last, as though it matters the least. And then of course you know what happens – everything but the creative work gets done.

Because I work in publishing, I also see a lot of material – and sometimes I think, why add more to the enormous pile out there if it isn't brilliant. I don't think I am brilliant, so why bother, there is enough stuff written or created that doesn't knock anyone's socks off. Those are the thoughts. They are not reality.

Thank you for reading.

All best, Annette

**

Hi, Annette:

Okay, so we have to change your thought patterns or else creating won't be available to you as a meaning opportunity!

I want you to begin saying several times a day, silently or out loud, "If I don't take my creating seriously I will have no creative life" or "Creating has an upside that does matter to me" or "My contributions will serve a purpose" or some phrase of your own creation that you commit to saying and affirming whether or not you completely believe it.

Your tasks for the next two weeks are to work on your mind (in the way I just described) in a daily, committed, disciplined way and to work on your project in a daily, committed, disciplined way. Okay?

**

TWO-WEEK REPORT

Dear Eric,

Thanks for this two weeks! Here is my report in point form.

WHAT I DID

+ I made time to write almost every day the first week and felt great

+ I finished boreal trilogy number 2, worked on number 3 and decided that I would write a book about the Shackleton leadership lessons told by a penguin (his name is Steve LPSB - Lead Penguin in Sensitive Behavior)

+ I made time for my creativity and said no to a few people, which was hard

+ My affirmation is "my creativity is unique and creating matters to me"

WHAT HAPPENED

After the first week I spiraled down, back to thinking that part-time, now-and-then, creativity really doesn't matter so why don't I just give it up completely, then I don't have to make myself wrong about it anymore, which takes up energy.

The second week I walked a lot (was off work) and did a lot of self-EMDR while walking. I realized that because I don't have everything else figured out, like where I am going career-wise and with a new relationship, that creativity seems like the frilly bit that comes last - and that until I get everything else figured out, creating is a luxury (my career or possible relationship are not in crisis – just not exactly sure where i am going – not a bad place to be).

This harkens back to childhood when I was a child and had a lot of responsibility, too much, and it's all I could manage (that was often a crisis situation). Anyway, I did my self-EMDR (bastardized version, as I am not fully trained) and walked and this cleared. A new thought arose – it's being creative that will help me figure out everything else, not the other way around! My creativity affects everything else, and makes everything else more fun, beautiful, worthwhile and easy.

My creativity began to MATTER!

WHAT HELPED

+ What really helped was knowing that during these two weeks I had a connection with you, even though I was working on my own. This was so important for me, because although my friends like it that I am creative, they certainly don't encourage me to stay home and create – they would prefer I go out, or come over to help etc.

+ Just continuing to show up day after day even when I felt I should just give it up. It's like the medicine wheel, up, over and down, around and around. If you expect that, it's no surprise and there's always an up after the down.

+ The EMDR and EFT helped. I think something actually cleared because after two weeks I am thinking the opposite of where I started.

WHAT DIDN'T HELP

Everything I did seemed to help. There was nothing I tried that didn't help.

Thank you, Eric! I feel so honored to be working with you.

All best, Annette

**

Hello, Annette:

That was a lot of progress! As you know, the main task for the next three weeks is to continue showing up in a daily, routine, regular way. In addition to that core commitment, what else would you like to include as part of your goals for the next three weeks? I look forward to hearing!

**

On the one hand we believe that creating matters. On the other hand, we don't. On any given day we can make an effort to believe the former or we can throw up our hands and believe the latter. Both thoughts are present in us, waiting. Watch out for that gesture of throwing up your hands. That is the exact equivalent of throwing over your life.

9. TEACHING AS CRUTCH AND EXCUSE

Most artists can only maintain a toehold on a middle class life by doing something else in addition to making art. That something else might be spending down their inheritance or their savings, marrying someone who makes money, working an onerous day job, creating some sort of business, doing commercial art or work-for-hire, or embracing a second career and becoming a lawyer, therapist, teacher, and so on. Each of these comes with a shadow side and its own array of difficulties …

**

Dear Eric:

I've been working in art for over 30 years, since high school, when I sold black and white pen illustrations to a florist for newspaper ads. I have a BA in fine art, major/minor in painting and drawing, and after several years of working in commercial art after college I went back to get a teaching degree, as an artist I admired explained, teaching is the best way to learn about art. Your students will push you to understand it from every angle.

LOL - it certainly did, but it also became a crutch and an excuse for not making art full time. I taught art at high school and college levels for over 15 years, starting with drawing, painting, crafts, ceramics and art history and extending my knowledge base to include computer graphics, web design, multi-media and online learning. During the summer I traveled a lot, doing watercolors and oil paints and participating in several shows, including a one-person show at a reputable gallery.

Over the years I have sold some fine art, but mainly my income has been through design and commercial work. I have become disheartened by my lack of success financially even though I know it is possible. My work in college and workshops was/is always at the top of the class, and my art generally draws favorable reviews from other artists as well, but I struggled with my purpose. I have sold very little art in the past and would like to see it become a reasonable income.

Your books and online workshops have encouraged me to find/create my purpose for making art, and I feel heartened by the fact that I'm finally aware of what I'd like to say, and why. I feel very discouraged by the challenges I face, as I have developed many excuses not to make art. I'm not lazy, but I find that I have a lot of resistance to creating art, and my habits have become dreadful. I hare off in every direction at the least distraction. Books are my nemesis, so I am lucky - no drugs, alcohol, etc. but Amazon.com loves me.

I have to carve away time each day to produce art, and I have to let go of my blocks to creativity. When in classes I have no problem, but working on my own each day without a boss or regular paycheck is proving to be a large challenge. As to my goals, at a minimum I would like to:

1. *Enjoy making art again*

2. *Make art every day for 4-5 hours minimum*

3. *Create a plan to sell art - a balance of online, retail and ?? that is simple*

My wow goals:

1. *Enjoy making art again*

2. *Make art every day for 4-5 hours minimum*

3. *Have a gallery show scheduled*

4. *Web site finished and retail site established*

5. *Sell at least one medium to large work*

**

Hello, Claudia:

Let me begin by asking a question, since you put as your top priority enjoying making art. Do you actually need to enjoy making it? If, for example, you attempt work that is perhaps hard or new or difficult in some way, you might not actually enjoy making it but of course you might make yourself proud by your efforts and you might enjoy "having made it" <smile>.

So I would like to double-check on your first goal: do you indeed need to enjoy making the art or do you perhaps need to set a different sort of goal, one like "showing up" or "making yourself proud of your efforts" or something along those lines? Your thoughts?

Best, Eric

**

Hi Eric,

Interesting question. I understand what you're saying, and yes, it can be enjoyable just because it is getting done - hard work is often rewarding for its own sake. The enjoyment is often finishing, or just taking the next step towards completion.

I suspect I've forgotten that making art is always fun, or rewarding. The pressures of making and selling art make it so much harder to relax into the art now that I'm paying my own bills. When I was younger it was easy to ignore everything else - I had very little to weigh me down, and forever to get serious about making a living. With a clean slate and no history it's easy to have a positive attitude.

As I painted yesterday I realized that I enjoyed everything about it - well, except for cleaning the brushes, though even that has become part of a very satisfying routine. It wasn't the best work, as I'm out of practice, but I know that with practice my skills will be good if I keep practicing.

I agree that setting a goal to show up every day is the key, so goal #2 gets moved up a notch. Okay, then:

Goal 1 - make art

Goal 2 - Finish 4-6 works

Goal 3 - Create a plan to sell art - a balance of online, retail and ?? that is simple

Wow list -

1. *Make art every day for 4-5 hours minimum*

2. *Finish 6-8 works - paintings &/or sculptures*

3. *Apply to two galleries or prep for applications, according to gallery schedules*

4. *Web site finished and retail site established.*

5. *Sell at least one medium to large work*

And I'd love to hear your honest thoughts -

"Wow, this is in group 2, with the ones who...."

Do you know that scene in Charlie and the Chocolate Factory when Johnny Depp is seeing the psychiatrist and he says "Wow, you're good" - I just had that whole scene pop into my head. How does it feel to be compared to an Oompa Loompa? High praise indeed...

**

Hello, Claudia:

Let's set as your two-week goals finishing works (as many as possible) and creating your marketing plan. If you want to add details from your wow list feel free to do so but make sure that at a minimum you start finishing works and creating your marketing plan.

**

Eric,

After a day of introspection, I'm also realizing that I have been wanting to work on less serious art - art that has a sense of play. Utah has a LOT of people who do amateur crafts and art in Utah is pretty strictly defined into FINE art and other, and most of the art here has a pretty serious approach, as Mormons are a pretty serious bunch. I think the next two weeks of work will be dedicated to that which is not serious. If it gets serious it's ok, of course - art goes where it goes.

Claudia

**

Hi, Claudia:

Are you saying that you are not intending to finish things and not intending to work on your marketing plan? Or is this an addition to those goals?

Best, Eric

**

Sorry, I realize we don't know each other well enough for me to add to my thoughts without being very clear.

No, I fully intend to finish. I think it might be good to include in the start of making art each day, but it's not the focus. I hope that it creates a less stressful way to anticipate the creation of art.

As my first set of goals had #1 - have fun making art, and you asked if it was necessary, I realized that I have been dreading making art because of the stress, and I need a way to break into the habit - to alleviate the stress a bit. At school we used to do warm ups, and this is the equivalent.

minimum

Goal 1 - make art each day (start with a warm-up)

Goal 2 - Finish 4-6 works

Goal 3 - Create a plan to sell art - a balance of online, retail and ?? that is simple

Wow list -

1. *Make art every day for 4-5 hours minimum*

2. *Finish 6-8 works - paintings &/or sculptures*

3. *Apply to two galleries or prep for applications, according to gallery schedules*

4. *Web site finished and retail site established.*

5. *Sell at least one medium to large work, or a series of small works*

**

Hi, Claudia,

Okay, that is very clear. For the next two weeks let's focus on your basic goals of starting with warm-ups, making art each day, finishing works, and creating a plan to sell the art. Please commit to a nice chunk of time each day for those two main tasks, the art making and the art selling!

**

TWO-WEEK REPORT

Goal 1 - make art

Goal 2 - Finish 4-6 works

Goal 3 - Create a plan to sell art - a balance of online, retail and ?? that is simple

Goal 1 -

I've managed to make more art than in the past few months, but not every day. I have worked more than in the past few months - 5 days total - with 5 days of prepping new work, cleaning up the studio area and work room. Unfortunately this needs to be done before I work on the next sculpture. The work done has gone well.

Goal 2 -

I have finished 3 new works in the past 2 weeks, all oil paintings, and started on 3 more. I've also done two small watercolors and a few sketches from painting outdoors with my friend Rachel and my sketch journal. I am happy with my progress on goal two.

Goal 3 -

I have talked to a fellow artist who is selling well in our area, and she has made some recommendations. Facebook is a great tool for her, and she doesn't spend any more time than she has to towards marketing in order to paint each day. She admitted to not having a solid plan and says that she has no idea what she's doing, but her sales have increased steadily over the past 3-4 years. I have visited with her and discussed her web site, as well as painting outdoors with her one morning, and we have plans to do so again next week.

Wow list -

1. *Make art every day for 4-5 hours minimum*

2. *Finish 6-8 works - paintings &/or sculptures*

3. *Apply to two galleries or prep for applications, according to gallery schedules*

4. *Web site finished and retail site established.*

5. *Sell at least one medium to large work*

Wow Goal 1 -

Make art every day. - If I haven't made art each day, I have been working on getting the studio cleaned up and prepping new canvases, doing some plans for the sculptures I've started. The tools and paints are ready to go. I'm disappointed that I haven't actually made art, but looking at how much I've done in the past two weeks on everything - marketing, contacts, getting the studio ready and talking with Rachel about her marketing as well as painting with her, I realize I've done a lot. I have spent at least 2 hours a day working on some aspect of art.

I realized that without having a clean studio each day I can't jump into the work first thing. Huh. I always had my desk cleaned off before leaving for the day when I worked in graphic art, and somehow I let myself get lazy about not cleaning up the studio (in our home) to start the next day's work.

Goal 2 -

Doing nicely there, will be working on the sculptures today.

Goal 3 -

I am waiting to hear back from a gallery in Salt Lake City that is a good fit, though I realize that I need a lot more work to be successful in business. Galleries expect to have a solid portfolio and I have some work to do. I have been collecting and scanning photos and slides of works done in the past, along with sending out slides to be digitized.

Goal 4

My web site is started but not much has been done in the past two weeks, other than research on Facebook and painting a day sites online.

Goal 5

I have made contact with a doctor who is part of a group building a new facility and left my card, explained my work and need to follow up (it has been 3 weeks) with an email and link to my work online.

**

Hi, Claudia:

I think that there is a lot of movement and a lot of success here! I hope you feel the same way. My sense is that if you make a similar plan for the next three weeks you will continue "knowing what to do" and you will continue making good progress. So I suggest that you name your goals and make a plan for the next three weeks and proceed!

**

As a coach, you're likely to harbor two feelings simultaneously: that your client has made real progress and that your client has so much more to do. There can be the temptation to forget to congratulate your client on what she has indeed managed to accomplish before rushing on to remind her about all that remains to be done! A seasoned coach learns to do a lot more cheerleading, celebrating and congratulating than may come naturally, because clients are much more likely to push forward when offered carrots and not sticks.

10. DISAPPOINTING LYRICS

ON THE ONE HAND, HOW HARD CAN IT BE TO WRITE A MEMORABLE SONG? ON THE OTHER HAND, IF IT IS SO EASY WHY AREN'T THE AIRWAVES FILLED WITH THEM? WHY IS ONE ALBUM FROM A SINGER WE LOVE MIRACULOUS AND FIVE OTHERS PEDESTRIAN? WHY ARE THERE ONLY A SCORE OF GREAT MUSICALS IN THE WHOLE HISTORY OF MUSICAL THEATER? SO, IS IT EASY OR IS IT HARD? FOR THE AVERAGE LYRICIST, FRUSTRATINGLY HARD ...

**

Hello, Eric:

I write and record guitar-based music. I've dabbled with blues-rock, classically influenced rock and progressive rock, pop, jazz, and jazz fusion. But primarily I like to write power-pop and progressive rock. Over the past decade and a half, I've put a lot of my recordings online (on free music download sites, not for sale), and received a fair amount of praise for them.

My main frustration with my work is that what I've created has all been purely instrumental. Now, I love instrumental music, but the audience for instrumental rock is limited - it's largely comprised of other rock instrumentalists! I really want to reach a larger audience, and to do that, I feel I need songs that have a sung melody and lyrics.

I've always struggled with lyric writing. My efforts always sound awkward and, well, un-lyrical. So most of the time, I don't try. Every few months, I think maybe the creative urge is strong enough for me to write a good lyric, but it never works out. Then I give up and wait another year or so. But the frustration of being an instrumental-only composer never goes away.

Early on, I naively and idealistically thought that the strength of my passion for music virtually guaranteed that I would be successful in a music career. Having studied violin for ten years, I quickly developed impressive (to my peers) guitar skills during high school. But once I entered college, my illusions were shattered.

Guitar technique and music in general were much harder than I'd realized. Like algebra, music theory intimidated me. I did pretty well in the music composition class and electronic music classes, but surrounded by so many musicians my age who were more highly skilled and who had already accomplished so much made me doubt my abilities. I felt I could never catch up, and therefore I would never be successful in music.

I graduated with an English degree and then got a job so that I could be self-sufficient. For the first few years after college, my main focus was in figuring out what I was good at, what I wanted to do, whether I wanted to get a graduate degree, etc. My urge to create music never went away, I kept playing and writing music as a hobby, but it was always a lower priority. I had stopped considering myself a "serious" musician; at best, I was a semi-talented amateur. As each successive decade passed, my goals dwindled as I allowed my career to dominate more and more.

For the next twenty years, with a few hiatuses along the way, I quietly generated and recorded musical ideas. A few grew into full-fledged songs, though - as always - lacking lyrics. Hundreds more are just isolated riffs and short sections of potential songs that, while deceptively captivating in and of themselves, I just wasn't inspired enough to develop further.

Today, somewhat dissatisfied by the work I do for a living, I'm re-examining how I might rekindle my creative hunger and get some 'real' musical projects underway. This Spring, I finally learned to respect my 'passion-o-meter' and allow that to guide me in what I work on and what ideas I pursue. By selecting only *the musical ideas that really excite me, I have found that the urge to develop them and actually *finish* songs is much stronger and more resilient.*

Since April of this year, I've been working almost every morning for 30-60 minutes on music. I am working on several songs, some newly written, others based on ideas from the past twenty years. Five or six are pretty far along now, and because I'm still excited about them three months later, I know that I'm on the right track. I'm still struggling with lyric writing, which is very discouraging, but I have faith now that I will prevail as long as I keep at it.

I think that my biggest challenges right now are:

* *Managing time: finding time - sometimes my work responsibilities override my creative time*

* *maintaining focus, inspiration, energy: whether it's exhaustion from working too hard or something else I haven't yet identified, sometimes a lassitude takes over, I lack the urge to create, and I doubt the validity of my artist-identity*

* *Getting past the frustration of lyric writing; maintaining inspiration and focus on developing this skill*

* *I'm such a novice at this that I'm still trying to "find a way in," to develop a viable approach to lyric writing. I have ideas about which I'm passionate, but the passion seems to dry up once I write a line or two. It seems that when I am working with language, I need to find a way to engage the creative part of my mind while not allowing the rational part to interfere. Most of the time, I don't have this problem with improvising/composing/ writing music; somehow, the wonder and excitement of the sound bypasses the judging part of my mind.*

* *During the coming two months, although it might not be realistic, I would love to finish three song demos to*

the point at which I would proudly play them for any-one, and would feel comfortable:

* *taking those arrangements and paying professionals (engineer, producer, musicians) to help me record them*

* *putting together a band to rehearse and perform these songs*

* *developing stripped-down arrangements that I and may-be one other person could perform at open-mic venues*

A year from now, my goal is to have nine songs, a full CD's worth, in that state. Two years from now, my goal is to complete a professionally produced CD of those nine songs, and to be per-forming those songs.

Thank you! Jackson

**

Hello, Jackson:

There's a piece here that seems to be missing, unless I am missing it. What about the singing part? You say that creating lyrics has been a great difficulty but you don't mention wheth-er or not these are songs that you want to perform yourself? If so, are the singing part (the voice part) and the performing part (putting yourself out there) also difficulties? Or is the idea that you are creating songs for others to sing? Can you clarify a little?

Best, Eric

**

Hi, Eric:

As far as performance is concerned, I definitely want to perform them, but I'm not committed to being the lead singer.

Although my base assumption is that the melody parts are for a voice in my own range (baritone) and that I would sing, if I find it too difficult to sing the melody, I would turn it over to someone else.

My egoistic investment is primarily in creating cohesive and compelling pieces of music that touch people, secondarily in performing them on guitar, and as a tertiary goal singing them myself.

I'm used to playing and/or singing in front of people as part of an ensemble - I've played in orchestras as a kid and sung in church choir for years. But solo performance is very difficult for me. To begin to overcome that anxiety, I forced myself to perform a song (not by me) a couple of years ago at a retreat in front of about 100 people. I'm proud to say that though it was hard, I did pretty well and received sincere compliments.

Hope this fills in the missing gaps.

Thank you, Jackson

**

Hi, Jackson:

Okay then. I think that is clear, though I think there are still some conflicts there <smile>. But we will keep it very simple. I want you to work on a song every day and continue on with that song for as long as it takes for you to complete it, however many days that takes, and then move directly on to another song, and continue that way for two weeks. Okay?

**

TWO-WEEK REPORT

Hello, Eric

I selected one of my more recent songs that I'm most passionate about. I decided on the singer viewpoint, voice, time frame, tone, and relationship between singer and audience, came up with a central metaphor, wrote down a bunch of ideas in semi-prose form, and began a brainstorming mind-map diagram around the ideas to see how they might interact and what other directions they might lead me in. The next step is to 'translate' those ideas into lyrics.

I allowed my day job to supersede my creative time for a couple of days (preparing to depart for a long vacation), then the vacation itself has distracted me from doing the work for several days. So I probably lost about a week. Now that we're not traveling, and are settling into a more regular routine, I've resumed my morning discipline.

Once I came back to the work, I realized that I was getting stuck again. I had gotten close to completing the chorus - the central idea of the song - but like always, after I get a couple of decent-sounding lines down, I can't seem to come up with a line that fits and will complete the stanza. I can't find a rhyming phrase that fits the idea I'm trying to express. Inevitably, if I try to make *that* line the starting place, and then adapt the other line(s) in the stanza to rhyme with it, I'm confronted with the same problem.

I'm becoming aware of the principles of lyric writing, but so far, these principles only serve to tell me what is wrong with what I've written - they don't help me write better lyrics.

In short, I think I'm trying to run before I can walk.

So, after yet another unproductive morning session, I decided to look for another book on lyric writing that might help put a fresh perspective on the task, maybe offer a new "way in" to the world of lyric writing. I found a couple of ebooks and bought them. One is very good, and yesterday I began working with it. But it confirmed my hunch that I need to revise my goal to something that is achievable.

So I'm considering setting aside the song that I started working on two weeks ago and just working on the exercises in this book. They may prove fruitful in coming up with lyrics that fit one of the songs I've written already, or they might lead to new songs altogether.

That's about it for now,

Jackson

**

Hello, Jackson:

It would have been lovely if finishing songs had proven easier but at least we can celebrate the fact that you didn't throw in the towel but rather created a new plan for yourself and then embarked upon it! If you're comfortable with your new plan, let's consider it the work of the next three weeks. And if it happens that you turn to some song and finish it, do not forget to celebrate!

**

Is turning to a workbook and its exercises a retreat from the actual challenge of writing songs or a reasonable move? Our heart wishes that Jackson would stay with the song writing and not retreat. Our head says, "Who knows, maybe this will work for him." Given the hardness of the task, to write memorable songs, this may well be a beneficial outcome.

11. NOT CHOOSING IS ALSO A CHOICE

ARTISTS MUST MAKE CHOICES. YES, YOU MIGHT INDEED WRITE THIS BOOK OR THAT BOOK OR THE OTHER BOOK. BUT YOU WILL HAVE TO CHOOSE ONE FOR NOW! WILL IT BE THE RIGHT CHOICE? WHO KNOWS? IF YOU ARE WAITING FOR A GUARANTEE THAT YOUR CHOICE WILL PROVE THE RIGHT CHOICE YOU WILL REMAIN WAITING, FRUSTRATED AND UNPRODUCTIVE, FOR A VERY LONG TIME!

**

Dear Eric:

My creative career began in October 1998, when my daughter was born. I was newly married, with a 5-year-old child, and moved to the Netherlands because of my husband's career. I was not used to being a housewife. I had trained as a Clinical Social Worker, worked in a hospital, then entered the corporate world, and then began software training.

At first I taught myself to paint using Dutch books borrowed from the library (I did not read or speak Dutch, though South Africa has a similar language called Afrikaans). I began with drawing and decoupage. I started painting and in 1999 had numerous exhibitions and was accepted by a gallery and then another and another. The second gallery gave me a wonderful exhibition but then closed down due to lack of business. The third gallery was successful until 2010, when they too had to close down (sales were impacted by increase in sales tax).

Then we moved to Paris and I joined an online art gallery for South African Artists. I exhibited in Paris. I made sales from my studio and through my Dutch gallery. I upgraded my techni-

cal skills and gave lessons as well as offering creativity coaching. I wrote articles on homesickness and how to thrive as an expat trailing spouse. I formed the goal to return to developing and facilitating workshops.

Then we moved to London and I started the tarot and learned to do readings. I designed and self-published a tarot deck and I also entered and was successful with the Chelsea Art Society featuring some of my work over three years. I approached the owner of a vacant shop space and successfully set up a gallery, that I ran paying the owner commission on works sold. This business thrived. When this arrangement came to an end a year later, I hired gallery space and ran that successfully for two months.

I made sales from my studio, developed my creativity coaching business, obtained a Coaching Diploma, and then we returned to the Netherlands. All my galleries shut down; the building in which I kept my studio shut down for fire code reasons. I had problems at my next studio and had to leave due to a dishonest owner. I no longer have a studio and decided to focus on coaching. During this time I wrote and self-published a book, ran an Artist's Way book club, upgraded my Photoshop skills and gave private lessons, and wrote and self-published a self-help journal.

Due to health, financial and relationship problems, I have taken a break from trying to find a market for my art and have stopped promoting my coaching. At the moment, my health is settling well. My children are getting older, and in one year's time, we could be moving to another country. If it is a country my daughter can go to school in, we will go along. If it does not work out, I have to rebuild a life in Netherlands. My greatest challenges now are being in debt so I cannot take a studio. Having said that, I began my career without a studio. My passion is creating notes with doodle-art/sketches to illustrate the points being made in lectures and coaching. I have used this with a client who experienced transformations from sketching during coaching. A lot of my creative energy is being used to keep sane in a rocky and volatile situation.

What I would like to accomplish during these two months is getting a clear sense of hope and direction. I would like to be clear about what book to write. I have many ideas ... and need to choose one. I could illustrate a book I already wrote or work towards publishing it on kindle. I feel I want to start something fresh. I would be happy to illustrate an existing work that is already out there in the genre of self-help/self-study for creativity. A minimum goal would be to begin such a self-paced creativity course playbook or one on gratitude or a fusion. I want to have a clear idea of the chapters necessary. A wow goal would for it to really take shape and feel I could look for a publisher.

I look forward to working together and to building momentum.

Best, Sarah

**

Hello, Sarah:

Ah, you have done many things! That is wonderful but that is also its own sort of problem because now you have so many ideas and experiences from which to draw. I find it very hard as I read what you wrote to discern what might be a commercially viable project from the many potential projects you name. As you know, not so many of the things you've tried have earned money and I am guessing you would like to pick something that has a decent chance of earning some money, as well as proving personally rewarding.

I wonder if you could "think this through" one more time and present me with a list of three projects (from among the ones you mention and maybe from among new ones too) that you think have a decent chance of earning some "real money." If you're willing, present me with that list and also include why you think each project has a chance of making some money and (if you can predict) what you would do to market it.

Best, Eric

**

Dear Eric:

I am thinking that to focus, I want to write. While I am passionate about doodling and sketching and so forth, I think I will begin by presenting my book in a format that is suitable for kindle publishing and take it from there. I have three possible books I could work on.

The first book is one I wrote for the espresso machine printing press at the American Book Center in the Hague. I printed a first copy. The cover was a challenge so I created a simple beautiful cover but eventually this can be better. I will design a new more creative and interesting cover. I will also begin editing it myself. When the book gets an ISBN here, a certain bookshop will put it on their blog, in their newsletter and also their shop in Amsterdam. It will soon be able to be printed all over the world, so for example, if I move to Munich and am giving workshops there, it can be printed there.

I also have an idea for a book that has attracted me since a good few years ago. It can reach a wider audience than my other works. This will be a playbook/workbook with daily activities/tasks. I have not written this at all so would be starting from scratch. I think it would have great viability as this system I would write about is said to be the foundation of The Secret but this project feels overwhelming, stimulating and exciting.

The hero's journey is another one of my passions. I started a blog on this topic eight years ago and it is widely followed. For the last year, I have neglected it. This is partly because I created a system out of it and struggled to find a simple way to present it. I presented it in parts as a blog allows one to do and I have a huge number of readers; I presented it in London in the tarot group there and have even received mail from people who looked forward to my posts. I have not started writing this book but am willing to do so.

Looking at this, my book about expat life does seem to have promise in my immediate environment. But then, if I move, I would do all the marketing and leave. Most of the benefit would be in running workshops based on the book and I should charge for them. If I give something free, it would be individual sessions and on a specific chapter. These expats may then be interested in a workshop. It would also be easy to enter into my new communities in new countries as international schools and clubs would be a point of entry.

Thank you very much for your help. You have already helped me gain clarity and I feel less overwhelmed already.

Regards, Sarah

**

Hello, Sarah:

Okay! I don't have enough knowledge to know which of these three is "really the best" for you to tackle but what I want you to do is to CHOOSE ONE of them and work on it daily and diligently! Choose one and then don't second-guess yourself about whether or not you made the right choice, just work on it a lot for the next two weeks and then we will see where we are!

**

Dear Eric:

Progress is going well on my book. I have been able to stay focused in spite of challenging circumstances. I coped by reminding myself that I need to return to myself and practice extreme self-care, meditation and keep up my practices of incantations, journaling and more (e.g. getting enough sleep).

I have invested some time working on the covers for the book, both back and front as well as putting some effort into reworking the blurb on the back cover to make it clearer and more attractive, focusing on the benefits to the client. I have also changed the subtitle and was pleasantly surprised to see how much better it flowed into the book.

I have started editing the first chapters, picked up small things to correct and even have been benefiting from my own 'course'! A big development is that after 'shelving' my book, I am reconnecting to how wonderful it was writing it and I see that it can benefit others and needs to be shared. In other words, I have reconnected with my purpose. I have invested more meaning into this project, by practicing mantras and affirmations from my book, to enhance my life but also as mental preparation for talking about the book and marketing the book and I am even considering running a workshop or coaching sessions before I leave the Netherlands next summer.

Again, many thanks. I can't believe how I put my book aside and am so pleased that it has been so easy to pick it up daily and focus on it and my plans for the book. This has flowed into other areas of my life and I feel more optimistic and focused, even hopeful all around.

Kind regards, Sarah

**

Hi, Sarah:

This is great! I think that all I want to suggest is that you continue, reminding yourself, when you have any doubts or resistance or life disruptions, of how good this project feels and how much you want to complete it. My simple advice is to continue doing what you are doing for the next three weeks and then report again.

**

Most people who have a million projects in mind have no projects in reality. It is a very rare person, if anyone, who can work on seven symphonies or nine books simultaneously. The mind really wants to work on one thing at a time, biting into that creative problem deeply, productively obsessing about it, and bringing it to excellent completion. When a client says that she has so many projects she might be working on, my response is always some variation of "you must choose and pick one." That seeming diminution and limitation turns in reality into the expansiveness of actual creativity.

12. I PREFER FLYING UNDER THE RADAR

MANY FOLKS NOWADAYS ARE INTERESTED IN PENNING THEIR MEMOIR. MAYBE THEY WANT TO HEAL, MAYBE THEY WANT TO PROVIDE A CAUTIONARY TALE, MAYBE THEY CONSIDER THEIR LIFE AS INTERESTING AS ANY NOVEL, OR MAYBE THEY HAVE MANY MOTIVES. WHATEVER THEIR STARTING POINT MAY BE, THEY OFTEN COME TO A STANDSTILL BECAUSE THEY ARE ACTUALLY IN SIGNIFICANT CONFLICT: PART OF THEM WANTS THEIR STORY TOLD AND PART OF THEM, OFTEN THE LARGER PART, DOES NOT WANT TO AIR THEIR DIRTY LINEN, UPSET FRIENDS AND RELATIVES, AND RISK THE DANGERS OF BEING SEEN AND KNOWN. IT IS VERY HARD TO WRITE YOUR MEMOIR WHEN YOU ALSO WANT TO "FLY UNDER THE RADAR"!

**

Hello, Eric:

I have 80,000+ words written on my first book project. I think I have another 10,000-15,000 words left to write to complete my first draft. My current deadline for first draft completion is Friday, July 5th and for second draft (ready to send to my first reader in Tuscany) is Wednesday, July 31st.

I have few external challenges. I've built a life that supports my writing habit. I have six mornings a week to write. I have a thriving coaching/counseling practice where I see 16-19 clients a week. Even though my practice is located in a big integrated health clinic (my associates are naturopaths, traditional Chinese doctors, acupuncturists), the majority (if not all) of the folks who come to talk to me are artists! (The magic & mystery of this fact is never lost on me.)

My greatest challenge is anxiety. I've developed a ritual around my morning meaning check-in and writing practice that works. However, the closer I get to finishing the manuscript the more I get seduced into being distracted. I think having an accountability partner is what's needed now. And I want to learn more about how to navigate the publishing world: How do I find the right editor? Do I need an agent? Do I self-publish first without even trying to interest a publisher? Or do I learn the game of sending my book to a publisher?

During this coming period it'd be fabulous to see what I have, re-write and polish the manuscript so I can send it to my first reader in Tuscany, then hire an editor and begin taking steps toward publication.

Thanks! Paula

**

Hi, Paula:

What is the anxiety about, do you think? Is it about "doing a good job" with the book as it nears completion? Is it about not really knowing how to complete it? Is it worry about publishing and the marketplace? Is it worry about the book's reception and what it will reveal about your life? Is it something else entirely? I wonder if you could calmly and patiently <smile> try to get at what the anxiety is really about and let me know your thoughts? It may be that something significant is in the way of you finishing this book and it would be great for us to know what that is!

Best, Eric

**

Hi Eric,

When I read your questions, I felt the rising tide of anxiety! So, I've spent some time "feeling into it" through stream of consciousness writing. Here are the useful bits (I think):

The deeper I go into creative mode, the more worried I get.

I'm afraid I'll get lost and not make it back to my "real" life.

I'm afraid this book will change everything.

I worry that I'm not ready for the level of expectation that will come with sharing my story with others in this way. I'm not a public person. Even though I grew up winning all the oratory awards with speeches I wrote and delivered, even though I was chosen to be the valedictorian of my high school class and my speech was a huge success, even though I did the same thing and won the same awards throughout my college years, even though I talk with folks all the time and tell them bits of my story to help them awaken to bits of their own story, even though I have a lot to say and I'm not afraid of saying it, I just feel this rising tide of fear.

I prefer flying under the radar and keeping a low profile.

The only thing that has ever motivated me is the desire to help people.

I fear that folks will think I know more than I do. I know only my own life. And I'm inspired to share it in the hope of helping folks. But I am loathe to be categorized as a "self-help" author even though it has recently become apparent to me that my book is not only memoir, it's a kind of helping book. I am still surprised by this realization. And a part of me wishes it were something different. The book is what it is.

I fear that I still don't fully understand my own story and if I'm unable to complete it then that must mean there are still unconscious bits I'm needing to become aware of before I dare to share it with the world in this public way. Maybe this is a convoluted way of saying I fear it is not good enough?

I'm afraid I'll lose control of my life. It'll get too big too fast. This is a very familiar feeling ... like my wagon is on the road but

I've always got one wheel in the ditch. Like the train has left the station and is careening down the tracks and I want to stop the train, step out of the engine, walk down the length of the tracks and make sure everything is okay before I continue.

I know from writing my story that I've traumatized myself in the past through the choices I've made and the situations I've created. That's not an easy thing to see. And maybe knowing this is causing me to be somewhat tentative. Because I like the life I have created now. I am content. Why would I risk it?

Why would I risk it? Because the impulse to write and publish never leaves me. And if I don't follow through, then it'll be like dying with my song still in me. And the bigger truth is that I'd never be content to stay where I am. That would be ultimately boring! It's just one book. I know now there are more to come.

It feels like taking the lid off Pandora's Box!

**

Before I could reply, Paula wrote:

Dear Eric:

Something just happened.

I'm writing about my third marriage and second pregnancy. And these words spill onto the page: "You've been wrong in your life before, but never as wrong as you are in this situation. The lovely Arab man withdraws completely. He doesn't call. He doesn't answer your calls. You leave messages with Ibrahim but you never get responses. You have such anxiety rising in you ..."

And something connects in my psyche.

I remember the story you tell about sitting with a man in a park and helping him to write his story from the inner place of being a writer in New York rather a man living in his war-torn country. Seems to me I'm re-experiencing past anxiety. But there's nothing "past" about it! "Get quiet and feel safe" is my way forward. I'll imagine you sitting next to me on a park bench …

**

Hello, Paula:

It sounds like the work is to feel safe even as anxiety returns and to commit to finishing this book even if anxiety returns. To that end, let's set up as the work for the next two weeks that you will write regularly, that you will endeavor to feel safe, and that you will deal with any anxiety that arises in some way other than by stopping the writing.

**

TWO-WEEK REPORT

Monday, July 8

*Wrote for more than one hour in the backyard under the Cedar trees. **737 words**. Feeling on track and proud of the new plan. No anxiety. None. Just ease. And the words flowed effortlessly.*

Tuesday, July 9

10:00 am I've been seduced into responding to "urgent" emails from clients today. What I thought would take me 15 minutes has taken me more than 1.5 hours! I know better than to EVER open my email before I write in the morning. I feel really sad that I've done this to myself. I notice I feel anxious, too.

11:15 am I've met my family obligations. Regrouped. Decided to ignore everything until I've written for an hour because I feel extremely anxious right now. I remember how good I felt yesterday after having written under the Cedar trees in my backyard. So I've packed up and moved outside. I've engaged the Freedom App and I have 60 minutes to write . . . no anxiety now.

Feeling proud of myself for having changed gears and made my writing the priority.

12:30 pm My world has been set right again. I've written **1,237 words!** *My feeling state now? Ease. It's as though not writing generates excess inner energy that turns into anxiety.*

Wednesday, July 10

All my words today went into my blog and my museletter.

I know I can manage this better. I won't judge myself harshly. Just see what there is to see. And move on.

Thursday, July 11

6:35 pm I've just written 436 words. And I feel my integrity restored. Because this morning I allowed myself to be distracted by the comments generated on my blog and the attending social media buzz. Which means I didn't write on the book project; I missed my writing time. Then my attention had to turn to scheduled client calls in the afternoon. Then family commitments. Now, it is the dinner hour, and I've declared that my time to write, and then walk in nature, is more important than making dinner. So I've sent my guys out for sushi and I'm sitting outside in my backyard under the Cedar trees writing!

And I know exactly where I need to pick up the story tomorrow morning when I start writing. Gotta say, I feel proud of myself for having taken a stand and walked my talk. Only 436 words but I feel they are key to keeping my momentum building.

Friday, July 12

Today ... 500 words. And lots of dots connecting in my mind about scenes I want to write. As though more memory is rising to the surface. Memory or story. I don't know if there's a difference anymore.

Saturday, July 13

Spent last night out with my beloved. Slept late this morning to steel myself for the next four days at the clinic. No words written. And I made the decision consciously. I need a break.

Sunday, July 14

Not a writing day due to clinic commitments.

Monday, July 15

I notice I feel exhausted this morning after two full days at the clinic. I also notice that I just cannot locate the mental clarity I need to write. What I need is to walk and rest and relax so that I can get to the clinic this evening. No anxiety. Just a kind of mental exhaustion.

Tuesday, July 16

I feel what I felt yesterday morning only tripled!

I'm just noticing. Not resisting. And I'm surprised by what feels like mental exhaustion. I feel depleted. And I'm wise enough to know what I need: walking, resting, replenishing ...

It's now early afternoon and I feel like I could settle in for a good write, but it's time to head back into the city clinic.

I notice the anxiety that I feel now is about **not writing**. I also notice I am resisting going into the clinic which is exacerbating the anxiety. I need to let go and flow because I have commitments I must meet. Writing will not happen today. It makes me sad. And frustrated. I won't be back home till late evening.

Wednesday, July 17

Early morning ... I am claiming this day to get back into write/right mode.

Coffee and toast in bed (after a grounding meditation), door closed, my family knows I need to be left entirely alone.

Except for Dante, our dog, who is curled on the floor in the room with me. I'm whacked out from the city clinic.

I will write. Not on my blog even though it is a blogging day but on my book.

My window open, I see the 200- year-old Cedar tree just a few feet away from where I sit with my Macbook. The fresh air sweeping through the room feels wonderful. The stillness exquisite. I am home. And I remember the words Margaret Atwood posted on Twitter several months ago: **Into the Writing Burrow now. Do not check email. Do not surf news. In! Now!**

Late morning ... I just checked my scrivener stats. My session target today was 1,231 words and I've written 1,233 ... curious how that unfolded.

I'm feeling restored. I'll break now and come back a little later.

All my bits are in order now.

Thursday, July 18

It's noon and I've written 1,447 words.

Friday, July 19

9:47 am ... 1,122 words in 45 minutes ... the story is rushing forth ... effortlessly. Feels like I'm flying!

10:07 am ... 1,395 words

Saturday, July 20

Not a writing morning this week ...

Sunday, July 21

Not a writing morning

Monday, July 22

Again, I'm whacked out from a full weekend of clinical work. Mentally exhausted. No words.

Total word count is now 89,148. My aim was to reach 90,000 in these two weeks. I've discovered there is more to write ... much more ... so new targets will need to be set for writing to commence tomorrow morning, Tuesday, July 23

**

Hi, Paula:

It sounds like three things are true, that your day job is real and exhausting, that there is a lot of writing left to do, and that when you feel "up to" writing it goes very well! Let's take these three ideas and make a simple plan: that you accept that sometimes you are exhausted and can't write and that must be okay; that you accept that there is more work to do and that however much work is required is okay; and that you are committed to the writing! Let us keep it that simple, shall we?

**

A quick reply email from Paula:

Hi Eric,

I love this. I thrive in simplicity.

For the record, this is a breakthrough. Acknowledging these three things feels right and true. And not resisting what is true is very good medicine for me.

*It's a real relief for me to see that it's not just a matter of me avoiding writing or being creatively blocked from writing. And that the anxiety that gets generated in me is actually about **not writing** due to being exhausted by my clinical work. And that that **must be okay.** Because that poses a very different kind of context for me in relationship to building my life.*

I will create a plan, as you've suggested, in the next couple of days. This past two weeks has been very productive for me. I feel as though my commitment to the writing has deepened and the foundation I'm building my future on has been strengthened.

Thank you, Eric.

With Gratitude, Paula

**

This sounds promising, doesn't it? And yet it remains to be seen if Paula is really willing to appear on the radar. It is easy to suppose that as she gets nearer to completing her memoir new and perhaps very virulent anxiety will again arise. It may even feel completely unsafe to put her memoir out into the world, even though that has always been her intention. If showing and publishing her memoir begins to feel that dangerous, Paula will need to stop everything and have a very difficult conversation with herself: does she or doesn't she want to accept the risk of exposure and the risk of pushback that every memoirist faces? That conversation may still be coming ...

13. THE HOLY GRAIL OF FORMULAS

FOR CREATIVE AND PERFORMING ARTISTS, THE INNER CHALLENGES THEY FACE HAVING TO DO WITH SELF-DOUBT AND A LACK OF CONFIDENCE OFTEN PLAY THEMSELVES OUT AS A DAILY HUNT FOR THE HOLY GRAIL OF FORMULA: A HUNT FOR THAT ONE PIECE OF INFORMATION, THAT ONE PIECE OF ADVICE, THAT ONE INSIGHT, THAT WILL TURN THEIR MESSY, INCOMPLETE WORK INTO SOMETHING BEAUTIFUL. THEY ASK OF THE WORLD, "PLEASE, TELL ME WHAT TO DO!" THE WORLD PROVIDES THEM WITH ANOTHER BOOK OF ADVICE, ANOTHER WORKSHOP, ANOTHER SET OF HINTS AND TIPS, AND THEY REACH OUT – AGAIN AVOIDING THE REAL WORK, THE ONGOING, PAINFUL, VITAL ENCOUNTER WITH THEIR OWN PROJECT.

**

Hello, Eric:

Though I'm Canadian my break in journalism came from an American magazine. I graduated from Rutgers with an MA (studied at Florence University) then did my PhD for 3 years at Rutgers in New Jersey. I finished the courses and took an 8-hour exam but I knew from watching the male dominated culture in the Italian department support its male students into professorial jobs and the women into high school teaching, that I would never get anywhere. I didn't fit in. I spoke up. I was offended by professors who read their lectures from 3 x 5 index cards, lectures that put us all to sleep. Would this be my fate too? Why had they lost interest in their field? I left suddenly, though I received a 4 on the long exam, and never regretted it.

Now back in Toronto, I tried to get hired by a magazine as an editor or writer. I struggled for years in soul-killing receptionist jobs that promised editorial positions but never delivered. I took courses on editing/writing/publishing but I couldn't break in. Then a miracle happened. Because I attended an art show in NYC and told a jeweler I'd love to write about her incredible work, when a magazine approached her, she gave them my name. I thought I was dreaming when I listened to a message on my answering machine from the managing editor of an American magazine, giving me an assignment.

I was in. I continued to write for her and four other magazines for the next decade. In addition, I wrote two columns and a book on an American jeweler who was a "rock star" in her field. I decided to stop, six years ago, before I burned out, and write the novel I always thought I would have already written by then. I'd written short stories but decided to write a crime novel set in Florence. I also made jewelry which I sold to14 galleries and I painted. I sold the first painting I gave to a gallery but now painting is on the back burner as I strive, in vain to focus on writing and finishing the book I started in 2007.

My "ups" seem to be all in the past: writing steadily for four magazines, writing two columns, getting a jewelry book published, selling my jewelry to galleries and museums in the US and Canada, and selling the first painting I exhibited. The "downs" are my present:

+ Lack of encouragement. Applied repeatedly for government funding to complete this book, since I have a track record of published work. No small feat, sending 50-page excerpts in triplicate to them and to ten small publishers as part of this process. No success.

+ Sent an excerpt to Crime Writers of Canada. Rejected.

+ Wrote short stories for on-line lit magazines' contests. Time-consuming and discouraging.

+ Lack of solitude and focus, diminished energy and a brain scrambled by sporadic elder care and life events.

+ *Inertia. Don't want to enter my office. Lately, I wonder if I should continue. I have millions of words written, scene after scene complete and described as "powerful" in the three writing workshops I've taken to stay on track. These proved to be more procrastination than helpful. In November, I had successful knee-replacement surgery on my leg with Polio, which changed my life. I'd like to lay my lethargy at that door, as lethargy a common post-op reaction.*

+ *I'm easily distracted and prone lately to hours of late-night TV-watching and doodling. At 3 AM, I'm the most alert and calm. I don't know why I've developed this habit, when I know better. My only excuse is that after a day dealing with my mother or life events, I really do need to do something pleasant with my free hours. Nevertheless this is depressing me because I'm aware I'm wasting precious quiet hours.*

+ *Interruptions and loss of focus are my daily issues as my needs and those of my energetic husband's collide.*

+ *I share the care of my mother, who doesn't speak English, with two sisters. She's in a great nursing home, but her dementia makes her rage against her caregivers, so she's often unbathed, which is where we come in. She broke her wrist this week so it's been three visits to the ER (7 hours each) to deal with the cast she partially pulled off. One sibling insists one of us three be at the nursing home every day. The home is quite far, and the experience of being raged at is disturbing. I don't think we need to be there every single day.*

My minimum goals:

+ *To find the energy to go on with the book that's eating up my life.*

+ *To learn to deal with aging, its depressions and panics. I know that life experiences from a long life makes for inter-*

esting novels but hearing the ticking clock only adds more pressure and heightens the frustrations I already feel when I'm interrupted etc.

+ To learn how to deal with interruptions, temptations, noises of life, the summer tempting me outside after a hideous and long Toronto winter.

+ To reconnect with the adventurous woman I used to be and go on vacation by myself.

+ To not worry about money all the time and deprive myself of vacations.

+ To deal with the perpetual guilt I feel when I don't do things with my husband or spend too much time writing, neglect the housework because I don't want to stop writing. And I often don't want to start because I know I'll be interrupted or expected to drop everything for a chore.

+ To deal with the simmering anger with my husband who won't look for work.

My wow goals:

+ To free myself of this book, this burden, which I'm determined to finish, but cannot.

+ To get an agent and publish it.

+ To let go of the anger and resentment at my husband's retirement and his past decisions that have diminished our funds.

Thank you, Barbara

**

Hello, Barbara:

Despite the absolute clarity of what you have written I am

nevertheless not clear on what the problem is with this crime novel <smile>. (It is a "crime novel" and not a "mystery"?) Is it that there are "too many words" and you don't know how to organize them or make sense of them, is it that you don't know something about the plot, is it that there is something lifeless about it that maybe could be fixed if you could identify it, is it … what is it? Can you explain to me a bit more what the problem is with the novel, separate from the problems you are having with you <smile>!

Best, Eric

**

Hello, Eric:

You ask good, scary questions.

It's a crime novel: *it has a number of crimes, which a protagonist solves.*

The work never feels good enough *(though it's been well-received in workshops) so I keep changing the opening. Hence many openings.*

The subject matter is dark: *human trafficking, a newly discovered mass grave, containing possibly the 243 Florentine Jews supposedly sent to work camps. The protagonist lives in a Tolerance Zone (for sex) where prostitutes work. Is it too dark?*

Yes to all your questions:

+ Too many words (I'm confused about which direction to follow, having wasted time following too many tangents and having written numerous openings).

+ I don't know how it ends.

+ I may have too many crimes for one novel.

+ It has exhausted me, so I dread sitting with it. Sometimes

I feel my brain scrambling just sitting down to write.

+ While considering your question, the idea surfaced that possibly I'm trying to write a literary novel and not a crime novel.

Thank you, Eric

Barbara

**

Hi, Barbara:

Okay. We understand that there are many real issues with the novel that must be worked out. Let's set as your work for the next two weeks showing up to the novel every day for a substantial amount of time – one hour, two hours, three hours, your choice—and bravely figuring this all out. You must face this, you must make choices, and you must get it finished!

**

TWO-WEEK REPORT

Hello Eric:

My journal confirmed something I'd begun to feel. I squandered too much time reading novels and How to Write books, (looking for the Holy Grail of formulas, I suppose), which have exhausted and confused me. Some days I read a book a day.

After supper, I'd begun to park myself in front of the TV and watch more movies than I've ever done before. I hate myself afterwards, conscious that I'm numbing not stimulating myself, or looking for ideas on how to structure a story – which is what I tell myself.

I don't understand why I'm so insecure about writing a novel when I managed to support myself writing articles, columns and a non-fiction book, etc., before. Possibly because it's a detec-

tive novel, it needs to be structured a certain way – something I've had to learn?

I used the four days I had to myself, to tackle the piles of notes that were everywhere: dazzling sentences from novels, tidbits of info I might use some time, change of scenery, brilliant insights, etc. The piles exhausted me just looking at them. I read several novels, but I still hadn't sat down and dealt with the story. Just to repeat: the book was written in 2009 but I've rewritten it twenty times at least.

This week I sat down with it and noticed:

+ The story line was too complicated.

+ I had no visible antagonist (I wanted Florence and life in that city to be that, but it went against the rules of the detective novel).

+ The opening was dull because I'd altered it to follow the rules of the two online workshops I'd just finished.

+ I changed the opening scene (yet again) and wrote something I'd like to read (advice from how-to books), which excited me.

But I still can't just sit down and write for an hour. I feel as though I deliberately throw obstacles in my path: a book I must read or a tangent I feel compelled to follow that has nothing to do with the book (happens too often!)

For example:

I discovered a book about his phobias by Allen Shawn, which led me to read his father's mistress's book about their secret life together when they worked at the New Yorker, which led me to watch his brother Wallace's movie, My Dinner With Andre. Then I had to read about Paul Theroux and V. S. Naipaul's famous feud after a thirty-year friendship, keeping an eye open for writing tips.

It seems so important, though I don't know why. I read somewhere (in your books?) that being distracted isn't a personality trait and that I have to commit to the work. Is it that simple then?

Thank you for your time, Barbara

**

Hello, Barbara:

I think the realization is perhaps dawning on you that you must commit to sitting there and completing the novel and that you must stop (or seriously curtail) the things you are calling research or helpful detours or writing advice.

If you have gone through twenty revisions, that is a little perplexing and makes it seem as if you are "blown about" a lot by a new thought, a change of heart, a workshop recommendation, and so on. Now you must trust yourself and complete the book, come hell or high water, by sitting there for hours, making decisions (maybe hopefully final decisions), and working out the book by doing the work directly in front of you.

**

Who doesn't wish that he could snap his fingers and make this better? Neither therapy nor coaching has adequate answers for the problems thrown up by human psychological complexity. If Barbara continued with a creativity coach, that coach would cheerlead, coax, suggest, plead, applaud, and do everything a helping professional can do to change a person from someone who rewrites her book twenty times and is still far away from completing it to someone who rewrites her book and, meeting and conquering her demons, finishes it. The coach would try; the client might well also try; and the psychological reality of formed personality might still prove too huge a hurdle to overcome.

14. SOMETIMES I DO HIT WALLS ON PURPOSE

WHEN YOU CONSIDER THAT THE NUMBER ONE PHOBIA IN THE WORLD IS NOT FEAR OF FLYING OR FEAR OF SNAKES OR FEAR OF SPIDERS BUT FEAR OF PUBLIC SPEAKING—FEAR OF PUBLIC SPEAKING!—THAT SHOULD GO A LONG WAY TO HELPING YOU UNDERSTAND WHY THE WORK THAT PERFORMERS DO FEELS SO RISKY TO THEM. HUMAN BEINGS DO NOT LIKE TO EXPOSE THEMSELVES TO CRITICISM, REJECTION, EMBARRASSMENT, RIDICULE AND HUMILIATION. WE REALLY DON'T. SO WE SHOULD NOT CAVALIERLY SUPPOSE THAT BECAUSE SOMEONE HAS SPENT 10,000 HOURS PRACTICING HER INSTRUMENT OR PERFORMING WORLDWIDE SHE IS SOMEHOW IMMUNE TO THE ANXIETY THAT VIRTUALLY EVERYONE EXPERIENCES "GOING PUBLIC." EVEN SEASONED PERFORMERS CAN FIND PERFORMING HUGELY SCARY!

**

Hello, Eric:

I'm a physical theatre performer, director, and teacher, specializing in making my own shows, solo and with ensembles. I've been doing this for almost 30 years, beginning in college, and I've made my living in this field for the past 16 years. In the past 8 years, I've been able to reach long-term goals of touring my theatre shows, doing extended artist residencies, receiving grants, and getting paid to create new material.

But I continue to experience rejections, disappointing performances, and missed opportunities, often with surprise, as if they shouldn't still be happening to me at this stage of my career or at least should be easier to handle. Personally, my marriage recently ended, I have moved to a new state, and I am going back to school to get an MFA at age 49, potentially to be able to teach full-time (while still creating/performing).

I'm still wrestling with anxiety and subsequent procrastination and lack of discipline. My unhelpful creative habits don't seem to ever go away, no matter how much I work on them, but I am a bit of a perfectionist (albeit one with low standards). My business skills have suffered in the past few years because of not wanting to put myself out there as much, which coincides with a loss of funding in state arts programs that had helped me immensely up until now.

I turn 50 next year and am beginning to experience limitations of aging, including minor injuries and health issues. I now have to wear glasses for the first time in my life! And yet my most recent solo show is the most physically challenging of my career.

Going back to school at my age will also be a great challenge: having to write papers for the first time in decades, collaborate with other students, work in more traditional theatre styles, and go outside my comfort zone on a regular basis. I've gotten quite used to having a self-directed structure, and now I will have to learn again how to adapt to one imposed from outside (which might also be what I really need right now).

I have two major creative projects in the next two months already scheduled; one is to work as part of a group workshopping the movement for a major regional theatre production, and in August, I'll be working on my newest solo show with a director for two weeks culminating in a public performance. I'd like to have plans in place for obstacles that may come up for both projects, internal and external. I'd also like to put more time and effort into them and use them as opportunities to take chances, learn, practice, commit, surprise, question, and reinvent.

My recent move to a new city was a huge undertaking, somewhat traumatic, and exhausting. My daily creative habit fell by the wayside and it's been difficult getting back into it. I'd like to develop it more, as well as add daily writing, reading and physical skill practices to prepare for school in the fall.

Thanks! Ethan

**

Hello, Ethan:

I think I would like to start very simply. Can you perhaps create a weekly schedule that includes all of the various things that you say you want to juggle? I would also like that schedule to include an hour or two a week of, what shall we call it, anxiety management or confidence building? Let's call it confidence building.

What could you profitably do once or twice a week directly aimed at boosting your confidence? Does anything come to mind? Let's begin there, if you agree: create a detailed weekly schedule that includes all the various things you say you want to get done and think on the question, what can I include on my schedule that would directly serve to boost my confidence?

Best, Eric

**

Hello, Eric:

Make a list of recent and past accomplishments under the heading, "I Did It!" Take some time to remember how I felt before, during, and after those accomplishments.

Make a list of actions along a spectrum from more to less confident, such as: make dinner (fairly confident); call cable company (less confident); go to local arts council office to ask for more information (retreat!). Work my way up the ladder, getting my strength back, and breaking down the more difficult tasks into smaller parts that I am more confident about. I'm sure I could ride my bicycle to the arts council office and back, even if I don't go inside this time.

Yesterday, I wrestled with making a detailed weekly schedule, procrastinating by spending half the day looking for the best app to make the schedule. Then I got stuck second-guessing how each day would be structured, not wanting to overwhelm myself and worried I'd just be discouraged by not following through. I finally made a list for the next day (today), with the goal of going through it, using the technique of working for 25 minutes, then taking a 5 minute break, with longer breaks after every four hours. I hope to get my feet wet in everything I'm juggling right now.

Each week is different for me, making it difficult to keep a consistent schedule. Last week I was in New York, taking a workshop in the evenings, and sharing an apartment with two others, throwing me off any work habit I had established prior. This week I'm home, with very little outside obligations, trying to regain a structure. Next week I'll be in D.C., working on a project all day with a group of other actors, and sharing an apartment and social obligations in the evenings. The next week I'm home again, catching up. I guess the weeks I'm home are when I need the detailed schedule most of all. But I also need a plan to use the free time when I'm away and time and place are more organized.

That's my report for now.

**

Hi, Ethan:

That is very clear—and very complicated. I'd like to make the work as simple as possible for the next two weeks. In addition to whatever else you must attend to and accomplish, I'd like you to each day identify one risk (like making a certain phone call or sending a certain email) and take it. See if you can do that in a daily way without drama or fear but just matter-of-factly. Identify a risk, take it, and done. Okay?

**

TWO-WEEK REPORT

Hi, Eric:

My risk today is to write this report, before my flight takes off. I'm starting to see a pattern of tasks that really aren't that threatening, but that I can procrastinate and then sabotage with doubts, so that they take much longer than they need to, with more accompanying stress.

This week I decided not to give that much power to these things, because they aren't that important to me. One example was a recommendation I promised to write. I was fretting over the details, trying to get it just right, when I realized it didn't matter that much in the scheme of things, and that just getting it done would clear the plate for more creatively meaningful things.

Of course there's no reason I need to get worked up about those either.

The last two weeks were full of daily risks, many of which I executed seamlessly. The difficulty came in deciding what my risk for the day would be, as if there were a right answer. Sometimes it was because the risk did not look like a risk outside of myself, such as making an appointment for a haircut, but felt like one at the time. Interfering thought: this risk isn't worthy of being called a risk. Other times, I questioned whether the risk was something I had to do anyway, such as to make a phone call to get information for grad school registration, and so didn't qualify as a risk. And sometimes the number of risks I could take in a day came flooding in and I was overwhelmed choosing, and felt guilty not choosing more difficult ones.

Last week was the most challenging, when I worked with a group of theatre professionals/teachers, workshopping a play at a prestigious regional theatre. This was full of experiences outside my comfort zone—it's been decades since I last worked on a straight play in this way—I don't usually even speak on stage! It was one risk after another, including having to read the play in front of an audience and with a major star of film and stage.

I kept going, kept facing each thing that came up and moving forward, until the last day, when I hit a wall (not literally. In my business of physical comedy, sometimes I do hit walls on purpose). Brainstorming with a group on a scene, I was put in the lead role to act things out. I got the sense that people were getting frustrated with my choices, and they attempted to choreograph my movements—I don't learn choreography well or quickly—which frustrated them and me.

Interfering thought: I'm no good at this. This led to doubts about me entering this MFA program in the fall, teaching movement to actors, and even doing what I've been doing for the past 25 years. I wanted to retreat, but coached myself to keep at it. I can only do the best I can do at the time. I tried to think what I would tell a student who had these thoughts and doubts, how much kinder and supportive I would be.

Finally I had to perform in front of everyone, and I perceived it as a big embarrassing failure, but also that I'd survived worse and it probably wasn't all that bad. When some in our group suggested we recast with another actor, I accepted without too much regret. I was better able to work with the new actor, and realized that he wasn't always able to quickly learn the skills I could do effortlessly; I had just practiced different things in my career. Instead of practicing dance moves, I had practiced balancing large bowls on my nose! I got through it, not feeling so worthless. Even setbacks can be used to build confidence.

Coming up, I have to start rehearsing my show again, improving it for a performance in August. I also have to get ready to start school right after that. Both things require continued confidence building and more daily discipline. I'm still not following a pre-established schedule.

**

Hello, Ethan:

If I am not mistaken you have actually done a beautiful

job on this "risk-taking" work and actually sound more confident! Congrats, if I am hearing that correctly <smile>!

I think that I would set as your goals for the next three weeks, in addition to all the real things that you need to do in life, the following two: that you "choose your risks confidently," just picking them fearlessly and without debating (as a smart, fretful mind does) whether it is "the right risk," "enough of a risk," and so on; and continuing to use as a mantra for dealing with risky-feeling events some version of "no big deal" or "nothing worth sweating over here" or something similar.

I think that you are actually making progress and I would love to see you make even more progress in the next three weeks, both in terms of "choosing risks effortlessly" and "not sweating much of anything." Keep your eye on those two balls <smile>!

**

It is illuminating that a seasoned performer who puts on solo shows year in and year out would nevertheless find it so difficult to make a certain phone call, even just to get some information, or so difficult to get a haircut! We are funny creatures who can sing an incredibly difficult lead role in an opera or perform the lead in a stage play and yet not feel confident hailing a cab or sending an email! Might it be that we spend so much of our human resources dealing with those huge performance tasks that we have few resources left over to deal with life's small matters? Whatever the reasons, this is the reality of countless performers: that the small tasks of life feel more risky than the big performance ones!

15. NO MORE SLEEPING IN, NO MORE AFTERNOONS OFF

AN ARTIST'S GENERAL DIFFICULTIES WITH CREATING ARE EASILY COMPOUNDED WHEN HE OR SHE GETS THE GO-AHEAD TO PRODUCE A LARGE NEW WORK. YOU ARE COMMISSIONED TO COMPOSE A SYMPHONY—YOUR FIRST SYMPHONY. YOU ARE COMMISSIONED TO PRODUCE A HUGE SCULPTURE FOR AN OUTDOOR SPACE—YOUR FIRST HUGE SCULPTURE. YOU SIGN A CONTRACT TO PRODUCE AN AMBITIOUS NONFICTION BOOK – YOUR FIRST NONFICTION BOOK. MOST ARTISTS, BUT ESPECIALLY THOSE WHO HAVE BEEN STRUGGLING ALREADY, FIND THAT THEIR INITIAL REACTION TO THIS MUCH-SOUGHT-AFTER COMMISSION OR CONTRACT IS PARALYSIS. NOR DOES THIS PARALYSIS NECESSARILY EASE ...

**

Dear Eric:

I am a painter and 2-D mixed-media artist, living in Massachusetts. My situation is this: I have a studio near my home that I have 24/7 access to. I make all my art here. I also teach art, both at the local community college, and in the summer, for one week, at a nearby Art Center. I have a lot of time to be in my studio all year round, because my summer course is just a week, and during the academic calendar for fall and spring, I only teach one day per week.

As for sales of my work, I've sold three very large pieces (16"-20" x 108"-120") in the last five years. One patron has bought about eight smaller pieces over the years, all completed before they were bought. I have sold several mixed-media pieces over the last eight years.

The most important piece I am working on now is a com-mission. I am setting up my own deadline for the first section of the commission-the panels. I want them to be completed and hung by the first week of September. There have been interrup-tions this summer, and I have also felt blocked by my own fear of getting started, particularly because I have never done a com-mission before, and I find it unnerving to be wondering if my work will meet my patron's expectations.

I have quite a specific sense of the imagery on the panels. Each will be a variation of a theme that first came to me through a series of rather mysterious spectral photos I took with my phone's camera the day before my friend's mother died down the street from where my car was parked. The spectrum appeared quite by accident in my phone camera's viewfinder, although I'm sure there is a scientific explanation for it based on the sun and the camera's angle, refracted by the glass of my car's back wind-shield. Upon seeing the photos, I had no doubt they would con-tribute largely to the commission.

As for my working process, I tend to work in fits and starts, except when I have a show deadline looming. There have been many dry months between periods of creative productivity. I cut down on these periods significantly when I started working on a much smaller scale, and often at night in my living room rather than in my studio. My mode shifted also in that the imagery be-came tangled and detailed rather than more geometric, symbolic and minimal.

I have found it very hard to get down to work before the middle to late afternoon, often only working after everyone else seems to have gone to bed. It seems easier to focus and feel con-tained by the time and space existing after people stop travel-ing around and/or calling on the telephone. An uninterrupted, even altered consciousness has been the goal, but holding out for that has also made me waste huge amounts of time seeking dis-tractions and taking care of "busy work," while waiting for the nighttime hour of quiet to arrive. The older I get, and the earlier

I wake up in the morning, the more impractical it is to wait until 9, 10, or 11 p.m. to start working.

The biggest challenges that I face now are not external, but rather, internal. I am temperamentally undisciplined, and disorganized. Both challenges feed off each other, and I become easily frustrated. One of the points that you make in Fearless Creating is to utilize extra small chunks of time to get creative work done, rather than always holding out until I have large chunks of uninterrupted time. Another tool you cover in Creativity for Life is having a creative writing practice first thing in the morning. I also struggle to deal with depression and anxiety in my creative process. I let both things steer me away from my studio, rather than tackling them head on with some very smart techniques you cover in all three books I have read of yours.

During the next two months, I would like to finish the first section of my commission and get it hung. I would also like, during this time, to start a drawing-a-day practice first thing in the morning, as a warm-up to my studio painting process. My " Wow, that would be great!" goals would be to commence and perhaps complete 3 Plexiglas sculptures, as well. And, if I were able to complete these, to place them in the house, in key positions where the sun would shine through them at different times of day and project the painted-on color to internal aspects of the sculptures as well as into different parts of the room, i.e. table tops and walls.

Liz

**

Hello, Liz:

As I understand it, periods of unproductivity have been a regular feature of your life, so your difficulty with working regularly on this commission is not really a new phenomenon, but perhaps just a more severe episode of what you regularly experience?

So our goal is not just to get this commission done—and done well—but to change your work patterns and to help you deal more effectively with anxiety, sadness, resistance, procrastination, and all the rest?

Please, if you would, describe your ideal daily work pattern and your ideal weekly work pattern; and see if you can name three—no more and no less <smile>--obstacles to beginning and maintaining that ideal pattern.

Best, Eric

**

Dear Eric,

Your observations, based on my answers to your questions, hit the nail on the head. I want to establish a daily and weekly schedule for completing the painting aspect of my commission, and then continue that schedule for the other two elements of the commission.

So an ideal daily schedule would be to get down to my studio at 8:30 a.m., five days a week, spend twenty minutes reflecting on the work I did the day before, perhaps write for another 20 minutes, and then begin the actual painting of the panels.

I would work for two hours and then stop for a coffee break at 11:15 until 11:30, and then paint again until 1:30. Lunch would be a half-hour, in studio. Then I would spend an hour drawing from life, and return to panels until 5:00. I would spend 15 minutes cleaning up brushes and then another 30 minutes looking at the work I had completed that day, possibly taking note in my sketchbook/journal.

Then I would close up my studio and go for a 30-minute walk before dinner. There is a chance that I could return to studio after dinner, but I tend to go to bed and read till about 9:30, and wake at 5:00, have breakfast, read or write until 6:30 and then attend an AA meeting from 7-8 a.m. So that is what a day of working would generally look like.

Weekly, I see myself in studio Mon, Tues, Wed, Fri, and Saturday, with the possibility of a half-day on Thursday afternoon. If I find that I work well in the evening, I might change things up a bit-take a few hours off on one or two afternoons to get other things done: go to therapy, hit another AA meeting, have coffee or a swim with a friend. Sunday would be my rest day. I go to church, a women's AA meeting, and often engage in some form of outdoor activity on Sunday afternoon. Sunday night would be another chance to go to studio and just observe my work, and perhaps take a few notes.

So, to identify three obstacles to carrying out this ideal schedule, I would have to say that they are as follows:

1. *Deep sadness about a 14-year relationship ending, and my need to get my belongings and maybe my cats out of the house I was living in with my ex-partner, and moving my many belongings into storage*

2. *Fear about beginning and sustaining my painting schedule in light of the uncertainty I have about what these paintings should look like, and*

3. *Needing to help my parents out with chores such as grocery shopping and laundry, and finding a place to live come September. (That's kinda four obstacles smushed together, but oh well!)*

Liz

**

Hello, Liz:

That is very clear. The obstacles, both practical and emotional, are very real, so we will have to take them into genuine account. Let's say that the work of the next two weeks is to keep to your schedule, just as you described it, while at the same time being prepared for sadness to well up, for fear to arrive, and for practical chores to arise. Let's call that the work!

**

TWO-WEEK REPORT

Hi Eric

I guess I would have to say I am embarrassed that I did not stick to my ideal schedule at all over the last two weeks because life got in the way. The three obstacles, and some other ones, became quite real. I had to go out apartment hunting (found one!), I had to go to several doctor and therapy appointments, I started working on my panels for the commission and then decided I really needed to wash off what I had painted and start all over by gessoing the panels first, which I am half-done with, I had several things I had to do for my elderly parents, and I needed to meet with my recently exed boyfriend to go over our situation and figure out what to do with my stuff, how to handle money issues, etc., and move some of my belongings out of his house.

I have been in my studio almost every day, sometimes just to look at the painting I had begun, and sometimes to organize the very large amount of artwork I have completed in the last two years. I needed to update my website, which I did. I also had to attend many AA meetings for my emotional health, and many of them met in the middle of the day. My AA sponsor, whom I met with, suggested that I create a do-able schedule to follow, rather than an "ideal schedule," because it was important to acknowledge all the transition I am presently going through, and important not to set myself up for failure, which I agreed made sense. That does not mean that I have abandoned the schedule I spelled out to you, but merely that I needed to be realistic about what would be suitable in my current circumstances.

I want to revisit the original schedule I set out for you and view it as what I am working toward. Next week I am presenting a five-day workshop, which requires that I spend the next three days in my studio and on my computer nailing down the syllabus for the workshop and also assembling all the materials. There are several things I need to purchase, and ultimately, I will be packing my car on Monday morning with 2 scanner-printers and four boxes of materials, along with an itinerary for my students of the week ahead. After the workshop is over, on the 2nd of August, I can begin my panels, which I will spend the next few days layering with gesso and sanding. I might or might not have some energy after the workshop ends at four p.m. each day to return to my own work in my studio in the evening hours.

I have kind of been all over the place, sometimes just trying to keep my head above water emotionally, and intensely aware that what I have been busy with is far from the ideal schedule of my days and weeks of art making articulated to you. Please don't give up on me. Some more self-coaching is called for. I see that now. No more sleeping in, no more afternoons off doing errands that can be better handled at other times. After next week's workshop is over, I want to give the schedule another go. I am more stable emotionally. I am serious about learning how to coach myself. So there you have it: a hopeful student, not ready to give up on your incredibly helpful teaching and coaching tactics.

Best to you, Liz

**

Hello, Liz:

I know that you can't help but think that you aren't "doing enough" but I hope that you will celebrate the fact that you are doing many necessary things and that you are keeping your life together, which themselves are no small feats.

Yes, you want to keep your eye on the painting, maybe by taking a deep breath and creating a disciplined, do-able schedule for yourself for when the teaching is over. Keep the new schedule simple, walk that line between "not enough" and "too much," and be optimistic that you can "improve" in this regard. You are doing a lot already! Yes, there is more to do with respect to your art, but keep the faith that you can and will do it.

**

On the one hand it might seem odd that a visual artist would arise early in the morning and, although she has no day job to stop her, nevertheless not get around to her art-making until the evening—if then. On the other hand it is not odd at all, given that a single psychological, existential, emotional, or practical challenge can cost artists their whole day. All you need to do is think "I am scared to work on this painting" or "I don't want to ruin what I did yesterday" or "I don't really know what I'm doing with this painting" and there goes the day! Billions of artist days are lost this way.

16. I LOVE GETTING TO THE PARK!

A HABIT THAT SERVES YOUR CREATIVE LIFE MAY ALSO SERVE YOU IN OTHER WAYS. MAYBE THE ONLY WAY TO GET TO YOUR WRITING IS BY GETTING UP AN HOUR EARLY, GETTING DRESSED FOR WORK, AND STOPPING BEFORE WORK AT A PARK TO WRITE. NOT ONLY WILL THIS HELP YOU GET YOUR WRITING DONE BUT THAT HOUR IN THE PARK MAY ALSO DO YOU OTHER WORLDS OF GOOD. SOUND FANCIFUL? LISTEN TO THIS BRITISH WRITER WHO GAVE EXACTLY THIS REGIMEN A TRY!

**

Hello Eric,

I write. At present I write historical novels. I've got two on the go but would be content to work on one during my two-month self-coaching course. I'd like to get it finished, or at least, end up with a really strong first draft. Before I started this novel I had quite a steady flow of non-fiction articles published, nothing academic, just little articles on hobby/general interest/self-help subjects.

I'd always wanted to write a novel, so I started one. I've written about two-thirds of an 80,000-word novel and have an idea of where the final 30,000 odd words should go. However, I've revised the first two thirds so much that now I can't bear to look at the finishing chapters. I'm sort of scared that it will be rotten stuff (compared with the first part). All of my writing friends recognize that there's a problem and leave messages on Facebook like 'Where's that novel?'

As to my challenges, I do have a day-job and work five days a week, but actually that's not the challenge. I have relatively few responsibilities at this stage in my life (I'm 58) and can certainly write for a period most days.

During this period I would like to knock my book into shape and move onto a fresh project. As a minimum goal, have a strong first draft that I could revise and feel inspired again to do it. As a 'wow that would be great!' goal, to finish my first novel, research at least one agent or suitable market to pitch it to, and do so. I'd like to end the two months feeling ok about myself as writer again - not pompous, or self-congratulating, just happy to be creating and sending my stuff out.

Best wishes, Emily

**

Hello, Emily:

That is very clear. Let's get this novel finished! Why don't you explain to me what sort of schedule for the writing makes sense to you? I would love it to be first thing in the morning before your "real day" begins but why don't you tell me what works best for you.

Let's keep it simple and doable – how about explaining to me which hour of the day you want to devote to the writing each day? Of course, doing more would be great!—but let's start there, with finding a daily hour. Which hour shall it be?

Best, Eric

**

Hello Eric!

I've given this some thought. I work as a Clerk of the Court - if you've ever appeared as a witness in a court case I'm that person who leads you to the witness box and gives you the oath to read out. It's intense work and I daren't be late for it in the morning. However, the hours are set, 9-5. Unlike the work I did when I was younger and ambitious for worldly success, there's no preparation, no extra hours to do. So, I was thinking that I'd like to get to work an hour early, with a bit to spare, and write in the park that is opposite the court. There are beehives, and crows, and people doing Tai Chi. I think there could be a writer too...

Perhaps later I might be able to put in some hours in the evening, but I'm tired and drained after work. I think to begin with, my hour should be 7.45 am to 8.45 am.

Regards, Emily

**

Hello, Emily:

That's a lovely plan! (Oh, and create a back-up plan for inclement weather.) Let's consider that our plan for the next two weeks.

**

TWO-WEEK REPORT

Hi Eric,

Here is my two-week report:

Monday 15th July

So I got up and out an hour early, which was a terrible rush. Felt a bit rough but knew I'd calm down later. There was the most terrible crush on the underground due, apparently, to some sort of earlier problem on the track. Having started an hour early, I actually got to work 15 minutes late. Not great for a court usher, and no writing done. Deep sigh. However I did a little jotting in my lunch hour. Awkward, as the lawyer sitting beside me kept looking, but it's the first time I've approached the last third of my novel in ages. High five.

Tuesday 16th July

Today it was a bit easier to get up an hour early. Got on the train without any makeup and having had no breakfast, but

I made it - and I have to say, I liked it. You see a different set of people an hour early. People who clean the street, and get to work early because they man the security desk, or clean the bathrooms. People in orange security vests. I like it. They're much kinder than the city bankers I usually travel with. They smile. In the park, where I have agreed to work for an hour each morning, I start on Chapter 19. It's hard. I've lost faith in the last part of this novel.

Wednesday 17th July

I'm not happy with how my writing's going. This is the second day I've been in the park for an hour before work. I'm loving the park, especially the people walking dogs, and the bees, and the man who does T'ai Chi, but my writing is shit. Really shit. The plot is all saggy in the middle and I've made five attempts on Chapter 19 - how am I going to get a bearable rough draft done this summer? Today I've brought a book with me. I purchased it years ago, but never worked through it because my writing teacher at the time really, really rubbished it. It was only my second writing class and I thought the world of the teacher. So now I've decided to give the book a chance. It's called 'Outline Your Novel in 30 Days'. I read chapter one and start on the first exercise.

Thursday 18th July

I got out the 'Outline Your Novel' book in the lunch break yesterday as well as in the park. The barrister I'm working with this week noticed, but was interested. I rather shyly told him of my dream to write a novel and how it has a 'saggy middle'. He said that he always roughs his arguments out using a similar technique to the one described in 'Outline Your Novel.' I was impressed - he's VERY famous in the legal world.

Friday 18th July

I just love getting to the park an hour early. I can't imagine getting in later now. It would almost be like being late. Today I was watching this man who obviously works in a circus or a magic act. He was practicing working a full glass of water across one arm, then his back and down his other arm. He must have practiced at least 25-30 times during my hour. It made me feel a bit ashamed of my moaning about a saggy middle.

Saturday 19th July

No work today so I went to the seaside, to a place called Harwich. I'm starting to think that part of creativity is about space - because I knew I had two weeks in which to invest a good, unsullied hour every day into my writing, my faculty started thinking about ways to solve my creative problems. So, this self-counseling lark is actually quite wise, isn't it. LOL.

Sunday 20th July

Today I stayed in as I'd rather overdone the sun, and besides there were domestics to be seen to. However I did sit outside in the communal gardens of my apartment block to work on the novel for an hour in the late afternoon. It was quite lovely. I'm even keeping up with the schedule advised by 'Outline your novel' which is astonishing for me - I'm such a slow writer that the notion of keeping up with a book for 'prolific' writers simply hasn't been viable for me in the past.

Monday 21st July

Got in too late for the park again this morning but it hardly mattered because I went at lunchtime instead. I'm following my 'Outline' book religiously and it's like being immersed in a retreat or something, even though I'm getting on with my normal life. It's quite strange because I haven't, as far as I know, slipped up in terms of getting on with my work, or anything. In fact, an odd thing - I'm actually slightly more up to date with things like housework and paying the bills than usual, as if a part of me is satisfied by the daily writing. Or something.

Tuesday 22nd July

Got in early and went to the park. It was a joy. London still has temperatures in the 30s C, 90s F. That's hot for a city that *isn't properly adapted for it. Still, I have followed the program to the point where I've got a rough statement for each scene in the book. The theory is that I should now brainstorm this rough outline so that I'll end up with a mini plan to work from when I launch into the 'real' work of writing the last half of this book.*

Wednesday 23rd July

Today I did my hour in the park and in addition, I went to my face-to-face writing group that is held above the Victoria pub in Lancaster Gate. There's a long tradition of writers meeting in pubs in London, and it was glorious on this summer's evening. I really enjoyed reading and receiving comments, and was able to incorporate them in the outline for the last part of the novel.

Thursday 24th July

Today I got home from work with a migraine. Actually think I might have been overdoing the writing! Ha ha. It has been very hot in London admittedly.

Friday 25th July

Today we went on a Works Outing to the Oval cricket club. I didn't do my hour there, because it's quite a privilege to go to the Oval, something most ordinary people can't really expect to do or afford, but I did it in the garden after work. I am now at the point where I have to make a list of contents for my rough outline. I've done a huge amount of writing in the last two weeks.

Saturday 26th July

Went into town. It was absolutely chock full of tourists as there is a major cycle race running through London. Most of the streets were closed to other traffic and I was able to do my hour sitting by the road, with cycles whizzing past. I've really learned to write anywhere and everywhere!

Emily

**

Hello, Emily:

That's great news! Really. That's a lot of progress, making serious changes to your routine and paying that much attention to your novel, saggy middle and all <smile>!

I hope that you'll continue and make a simple, useful plan for the next three weeks, keep to it as best you can, and at the end of those three weeks report to me on what's transpired. If you think you would find that useful, please proceed that way and report in three weeks!

Excellent work!

Best, Eric

**

Learning to write "out in the world" can make a huge difference in a writer's life. Suddenly you aren't restricted to a certain space or a certain time of the day or a certain way of being. I am writing this at the airport—why wouldn't a writer write at the airport? Or riding on a bus? Or sitting by the shore? If you feel weird and conspicuous writing in the world make dealing with that sense of weirdness and conspicuousness one of your self-coaching goals. Every park bench can be your writing haunt!

17. HOW DISAPPOINTING THAT ART IS A BUSINESS

YOU START OUT, GET LUCKY, GET GALLERY REPRESENTATION EARLY AND SELL YOUR FIRST PAINTINGS. THEN THE ART MARKET COLLAPSES AND GALLERIES FOLD RIGHT AND LEFT? WHAT THEN? YOU CAN WISH THAT NOTHING HAD CHANGED—BUT IT HAS! YOU CAN WISH THAT THE BUSINESS OF ART HAD NOT GOTTEN INFINITELY HARDER FOR YOU—BUT IT HAS! MOST CREATIVE AND PERFORMING ARTISTS HAVE GRAVE DIFFICULTIES WITH THE MARKETPLACE BUT THE ARTIST WHO HAS HAD SOME EARLY SUCCESS FACES A POIGNANT SPECIAL DIFFICULTY, THAT SHE HAD SOMETHING AND "LOST" IT. AND DOESN'T LOSS HURT?

**

Hello, Eric

I am a mixed media painter working on panel, paper and mylar. I am also a printmaker working mostly with monotypes. My work is abstract and gestural in nature, using my internal imagery as source material. I attempt to work without preconceived ideas and follow process.

I have always been interested in the subconscious and how it can be expressed, or made visible, through the process of art making. I work intuitively, responding to what is there, and allow accidents and mistakes to remain as evidence of my journey with the work. I use various techniques and materials to create surface marks: drawing, scratching, abrasion, erasure, transferring and layering.

I graduated from a fine arts program in 2004 when I was in my forties. It was a lifelong dream fulfilled to attend an arts pro-

gram and begin working as an artist full time. I was a recognized student and received a lot of encouragement for my work. Upon graduation I was immediately offered representation by one of the leading contemporary art galleries in our city. It had been well established as "the" gallery to be in if you were a contemporary painter and I was in very good company, and feeling slightly intimidated, but excited by my future.

The gallery owner sold several pieces of my work and I had two successful shows with her before she retired, sold the building and closed the gallery that had been a fixture in our arts community for over 25 years. I had been with her for just over two years before she closed and, truthfully, didn't know of another gallery I wanted to be in - she was it, for me.

I decided to work at self promoting and joined a local studio tour which required the participating artists to open their studios twice a year, once for 10 days in the summer and then for 4 in the late fall. I have been a member of this tour since then, although this year I am on sabbatical as I've relocated my studio space and have had issues with producing work. The first few years on the tour I did very well, sold quite a bit of work and had excellent feedback. Then with the recession in 2008, sales slowed down for all the artists and it has been a real struggle to justify the work that we put in to running, promoting and "enduring" the 10 days of open studio time.

During that time I did find another gallery in my area to represent me. I was there for about two years and then she closed her doors due to lack of business. The owner liked my work very much and the working relationship we had was good, just very few sales during the time I was there.

I also secured a gallery in Toronto in November 2011. This was a new gallery and I decided, upon reviewing their contract and speaking with the manager, to take a risk on a gallery with no proven track record. Unfortunately, over the last year and a half they did not sell any of my work and recently closed their *doors also. The manager left several months ago and the owners stopped communicating with the artists.*

Currently, I am no longer represented by any galleries and after this last experience, I'm not sure I want to be. It had always been the goal to get several galleries across the country to represent my work. Now I'm unsure that this goal is worthwhile, and if it isn't then what replaces it?

My biggest challenges right now in my creative life are multi-layered. I have the obvious external challenge of how to get my work sold. Do I continue to look for "good" galleries at a time when many are closing and take the risk of losing my work, or spending more money to ship pieces across the country to galleries that I can not monitor well because of the distance. It seems the art world is changing significantly right now and the traditional brick and mortar gallery may not survive this new virtual world. I find it hard to have faith in this as a path when I hear so many stories and have had such unsuccessful experiences of my own.

The other challenge is less clear to me, more internal. Why am I not interested in working right now, especially after such a long absence? I am involved with a new arts center and the demands on my time because of this involvement, along with the preparation for the annual summer studio tour, meant that I was doing everything except making my art. I could find very little quiet time for myself to drop into the space to work from. I feel disconnected from my art making, my purpose and have a feeling of meaninglessness around the work. I've had long breaks from working before and have always just started right back up when I wanted to. Knowing that I will feel tension and angst at first, I often start with small, less precious work to loosen myself and generate the creative juices. Working brings more work and every time I had successfully navigated this impasse of not working, I felt certain that I could always find my way back. This time it feels different and I'm not sure why.

Then there is the internal/external struggle of making a living from my work. I am, gratefully, supported by my husband who makes a very good living at what he does. He agreed to support me through art school and the launching of my career ... which all seemed to be going well, up until the last couple of years when things slowed down. I feel tremendous guilt for not contributing to the household income and have considered doing something else to earn income for myself, but I'm concerned that I would not be able to make the work that I do or spend the time promoting it, that would be required to continue with an art career - then I'd become a hobbyist, not an artist.

Dreams dashed and all the time I've invested wasted. It feels like a double bind and I feel frozen, not knowing how to stay true to myself as an artist and contribute to my partnership with my husband. Especially when I reflect back on the past year and how I lost myself in the busyness of launching a new enterprise, the gallery, and how my work suffered. The space to create from eaten up with administrative duties and to do lists, my mind filled with details and clutter. How could art making and a second career co-exist?

During the next two months, I'd like to get some clarity around my resistance to working and free myself up to be back in the studio with a regular practice. I'd like to be working in a focused way, building a cohesive body of work that I could show, either in a commercial gallery through representation (should I feel confident in that as a direction) or through self promotion— that is, renting a space to host my own exhibition.

What would be wonderful is if I could find a way to work effectively at my art career, while earning a decent living through another source, with those two things being complimentary to each other. I wonder if counseling could be the supplemental career to complement my art making? I'd like to explore and answer some of these questions, getting clear on what is holding me back or preventing me from doing both my art and counseling.

Sincerely, Chris

**

Hello, Chris:

Let me ask a few hard questions.

First, as it appears to be getting harder to sell art, do you want to stop and counsel professionally instead? Is it possible that counseling is enough of a meaning opportunity that it can make up for the loss of art making as a meaning opportunity?

Second, if that is not possible or not desirable, can you paint a picture of what might motivate you to paint if it is not sales? That is, what could make art making a sensible, doable, and worthwhile enterprise if it didn't involve sales?

Third, if it is imperative that you sell, if that is the only thing that can really motivate you, can you create a real, concrete plan for selling your art in this exact economy?

Best, Eric

**

Hello Eric,

Thank you for these challenging questions. They have me really thinking about how I value my work, my art making, and this issue has been "up" for me for a while now. Perhaps this is why I am in a holding pattern at the moment, as I attempt to reestablish the "value relationship" to my work.

When I try to imagine myself not making art again, I feel a great sadness and loss. I don't believe that is what I want. I know that my art making is based in a very deep need to create that has been with me my whole life and I feel it is necessary for my wellness of body, mind and spirit. Although counseling is meaningful and would meet me in that place of self fulfillment that comes from doing service work, art making is a different sense of fulfillment. It meets me in a deeper place of spirit, where I have tapped into something other than myself, something greater. There is no other work that has felt as meaningful as art making.

It is this pesky issue of having to earn a living that gets in my way. I have always felt that the completion of a piece of art is the relationship between it and the viewer that occurs upon it being viewed in an exhibition space. I am very much interested in the experience that others have when viewing art, especially what it says about them. If I didn't feel the pressure to have an income, I would not give as much energy to the need for sales and focus on the creating and showing of the work, allowing those experiential moments to be the completion of a process that started with the blank canvas.

So, the truer motivation to make art, for me, is to share it and create an experience for myself and ultimately for others that witness the finished work. The viewers' choice to purchase the work feels like a tremendous compliment and a desire to continue this experience with the work, as it spoke to them in a way that was meaningful for them.

When I try to envision a second, complementary career to my art making, so that I could take away the need of having to earn a living from my art, I notice I get concerned about the time dedicated to the second business and how that would impact my art making. Perhaps this is just fear and not a useful way to direct my energy, but I have experienced myself creatively shutting down when I feel overloaded with demands and would be concerned about meeting exhibition deadlines and finding growth in my work. It feels as if being a strong painter requires full time attention and dedication and less than that leaves me with the real possibility of being just an okay painter, not strong enough for what I hope for. Perhaps there is a balance there I am not seeing. I am just finding it increasingly difficult to cultivate the space to create from in this busy, information age we live in.

Selling is not the only motivation for making art, so monetizing my work through a plan that might involve inexpensive reproductions, art cards, etc. has always felt like it was taking away from the work itself and was limiting my potential to secure a good gallery, as they do not look fondly upon artists that self promote to that degree. However, if I should decide to change courses completely and forgo the ideal of securing gallery representation, this maybe is an option to consider. Up until now, I've not wanted to prevent an opportunity for representation, by self-promoting to that degree. I had been strongly advised to be very discerning about the choices I make early on in my art career so as to not close any doors that I might need opened in the future.

It feels as if this time is all about reassessment and seeking a new direction. Since I started working as an artist, I've always made work for a reason: an exhibition, a juried show, a studio tour. I have not, as yet, made work without a deadline or purpose. I think I've come to rely on those prompts to push me into working. At the same time they have prevented me from exploring new ideas because the luxury of time was not there for that.

I am eager to find out what lies beneath my, very likely, limiting beliefs and find a new relationship to the work that is not so charged with the need for sales.

With much appreciation, Chris

**

Hello, Chris:

This is very clear but it also doesn't give a clear "working goal" for the moment except "more thinking." I wonder if we can add a second goal for the coming two weeks in addition to more thinking about these matters? I wonder if we can add the "simple goal" of doing the art for an hour a day "while you think"? I hope you'll see this as a logical pair of short-term goals, continuing to think and doing your creative work (which of course may be informed by what you are thinking!).

**

TWO-WEEK REPORT

Hello Eric,

During my two weeks of self-coaching I didn't manage to get too many hours in the studio. Summer is endlessly full of distractions and I'm easily pulled away from my commitment to "work" at my art. I did do some journaling about the feelings that were coming up around the "work" of art making. I have discovered some truths for and about myself in this.

For me, making art was to be my "chosen" career, a dream come true. In order for that dream to be fully realized I have believed that I would have to make art and only make art, meaning that it was not possible to make art successfully unless I was fully dedicated and committed, giving it all my available time and immersing myself fully. Every time I was pulled away from my art I allowed frustration to rise up within myself. I would be thinking things like "How am I supposed to get my work done with all these obligations in my way. It's impossible. Don't they understand! I need space!"

This frustration caused me to shut off from the flow of creative energy and became a self-fulfilling prophecy, as I would feel unable to work in the energy I was holding. I realize that it is up to me to create a space to work from regardless of whether the circumstances around me support that or not. I can shift my energy by shifting my internal dialogue and allowing for a more positive mind space to exist.

The other piece that I discovered is around my disappointment about art as a business. I feel that I have set myself up, in a way, to feel this disappointment by having an expectation that I "should" be able to make a decent living through my art making. I have allowed the art market to be the deciding factor as to the worth of my work. I felt that I was doing everything that I was supposed to do to put myself out there in an effective way and when the results of those efforts did not match up with my expectations, I allowed myself to feel hugely invalid as an artist.

As the economy shifted and art sales diminished I internalized a message that it is impossible to succeed at being an artist if I could not sell the work. Your questions helped me to see this connection more clearly and have helped to bring me back to art for art's sake.

So, I feel that my "thinking" has helped me a great deal to see more clearly my part in this cycle of self-sabotage. I now feel that I can approach my work with more of an attitude of play, rather than work. I plan to monitor my speaking around my art, especially when asked, "How is it going?". In the past I felt obligated to speak the truth about losing galleries and slow sales but today I feel that I need to focus on what is working and how I'm cultivating ideas right now and moving forward.

I have made a commitment for a studio visit in September. An artist visiting from the East Coast, who admires my work, has asked to see the work in person. At first I felt concerned because I haven't been working much at all since I moved my studio, but then I felt it would be beneficial for me to say yes and trust that I will be back fully engaged with my work by then.

Thank you, again, Eric.

All the best, Chris

**

Hello, Chris:

That's great news! Really. What a lot of progress! I hope that you will continue and make a simple, useful plan for the next three weeks, keep to it as best you can, and at the end of those three weeks report to me on what's transpired. If you think you would find that useful, please proceed that way and report in three weeks!

Best, Eric

**

If you are somehow truly an island, then you do not need to concern yourself with what is happening on the mainland. But if the goals you contrive for yourself and if the meaning investments you make involve the real world of other people, commerce, and the world as it is, then you must concern yourself with all that or change your goals and meaning investments. If you choose the former, deal with the world. If you choose the latter, deal with the change. Brooding, standing still and feeling paralyzed are not the answers. Either deal with the world as it is or make a genuine change!

18. FLIPPING THE SWITCH

MANY CREATIVE PEOPLE HAVE THE FOLLOWING EXPERIENCE. THEY FIND IT HARDER TO GET INTO THE "RIGHT MIND SPACE" TO CREATE THAN TO DO THEIR ACTUAL CREATIVE WORK. AS SOON AS THEY ARE IN THAT "RIGHT MIND SPACE" THE WORK FLOWS READILY: AH, BUT HOW GROTESQUELY HARD IT IS TO GET THERE! DOUBT, WORRY, NOISY MIND, RESISTANCE, EXISTENTIAL DESPAIR, AND MUCH MORE CONSPIRE TO MAKE IT FEEL AS IF THIS COULDN'T POSSIBLY BE THE RIGHT TIME TO CREATE. IF ONLY THERE WERE A SWITCH TO FLIP TO MOVE US DIRECTLY TO THE CREATING—AND IN FACT THERE IS ONE!

**

Hello, Eric

I am a photographer. I have been using photography to make art for nearly thirty years. It is in the last 5 years that I have actively tried to market and sell my art. I have had some successes, and a good amount of non-responses, many more non-responses than successes.

I somehow feel nervous about working the successes. I also feel slightly nervous around those who are interested in supporting me and/or interested in any part of my process along the way. It's as if I am being immodest. Success might not really be the right word here. I don't feel like I am swallowing these experiences whole, eating them up with abandon.

I feel like when someone expresses interest and it requires (as it almost always does) back and forth email or communication that I move slowly, as if every communication is a challenge not to fail on my part. I feel a little nauseous just thinking about it. I might wait an extra day to respond and keep it lingering like a low-grade fever, not jumping in with both feet forward.

Most feedback about the work from people or places I value and respect is really very positive, and more of a conversation. It feels like the work is taken seriously ... my work is in a good place. It has arrived in a manner of speaking, but that isn't easing any of my internal struggles. Maybe it is a mistake to think that it might. Maybe I shouldn't connect success or any accomplishments with the lessening of internal dis-ease or struggle at all?

My biggest challenge is the feeling that I just described and when it plays out fully I experience fear and ambivalence and more fear. It doesn't make sense that I will ever make enough progress with my art work given the energy this fear and ambivalence take up, and the somewhat slow speed at which I move the communications forward with those who are interested.

It feels like I am letting it all slip through my fingers, and looking at it as it happens. The challenges are to move through the morass more quickly, to not give it such weight, to give the work the weight instead. Maybe I should also give my relationships and my community more weight but I shouldn't also give them more energy through ambivalence and fear. It seems they have enough, take up enough room and need to be reigned in.

My other major issues are to make sure that I give enough time, weight and spirit to the artwork (as opposed to the commercial photo work and all the other things in life that there are to do). That again seems to be about intention and value. I need organization. Organization and specificity challenge the ambivalence and fear. Organization gives me actionable steps and moves my whole program forward. Perhaps I need a detailed outline of what I want to accomplish?

I feel that it is really important to make a palpable shift of intention towards a daily practice of art making and art promoting. I would like for the next two months to daily, actively see that shift. But how to track this is the question? Specifically, I think it is important to be actively working with my camera, on a daily basis. Other important things are outreach and conversations with art buyers, interior designers, curators and artists' reps.

I need to feel as if there is a place for my work, not just a drawer in my studio. I have some specific audiences in mind but I should probably name them more clearly. So, I would like to actively spend time doing things with my hands and interacting with subjects. I want to be away from the computer for this. I also want to actively spend time with outreach, and see results. How to see results and how to feel in myself, in my interior world that those results are helping me, easing me, meaning something to me? The process and the results need to mean something. Is that the right question?

Thank You!!

Best, Kellie

**

Hello, Kellie;

It does sound like you are quite getting in your own way <smile> and stalling yourself through –whatever it is exactly – nerves, over-vigilance, shyness, or something else. Let us work on getting you out of your own way!

I would like you to vanish and cease to be <smile> except as the happy, busy executor of your smart, updated to-do list. So, to begin with, let's get that list created (while remembering to stay out of your own way as you create it!).

Create a smart to-do list for the next two weeks that includes art-making, camera contact, and lots of reaching out, networking, re-contacting with folks, and so on, a really nice, robust, clear, concrete list of "the work to do." Let's see what that list looks like, shall we?

Best, Eric

**

Thanks Eric!!

I just want to clearly understand. I should be writing my to-do list for the next two weeks? Should the scope of this list be far and wide (years into the future?) or very close at hand (the next couple of months?) or be about both? Should I try to put into action anything on the list or wait for your feedback once you see the list?

Kellie

**

Hi, Kellie:

The list is about things you intend to do during the next two weeks only: create the list and then execute it <smile>! Keep focused there.

**

HI Eric,

It went well. It was a very busy two weeks. A lot of commercial work; or rather I did some commercial work that ate up a lot of hours. In general, I feel I was able to keep some of my focus on the art side of my work. I was able to do that better than usual. Not sure why that was because I did have a very hard time making a to-do list that was specific, that had a series of next actions and properly reflected/quantified the work that I wanted to do.

Maybe that itself is really the issue. Art making did remain more significantly in the front/consciousness of my brain, almost like a guest at the dinner table reminding me that they were hungry too. But I was very aware at the beginning of the process that I couldn't quantify the art part. I felt unsettled. Did not want to name things. Awareness of my art projects was present, but felt aimless.

Specifically, I was really very good about reaching out, networking and following up! I could make an actionable list on that front, about reaching out. I was good about generating meetings, following up, staying on people's radar and creating next steps that allowed forward movement on projects, and broke down large amorphous projects into doable steps. I had some inquiries that were unexpected and I followed up quickly. Some people have not responded (to be expected/this doesn't really concern me), some are actively in process and some are finished.

I have a piece that will run in a major magazine in September, which was a fun development. It was initiated on a Friday afternoon, some back and forth to find the right image, approval by the art director and then I delivered the artwork and invoice by Monday morning by 8 am. So that is a very clear success that I can name. In terms of reaching out I do feel that I am creating structure to work within and that is working for me. There are tangible results and I am creating energy and sustaining momentum.

I guess I would like to understand why I couldn't quantify my art making to-do list. I just looked back on what you wrote to me and as I just mentioned was very successful on the reaching out front. However, in terms of art making and camera contact, I was not so successful. I wonder why? If I had to come up with an answer I would say that to initiate that kind of work feels like I need to do it absolutely first thing, really in the middle of the night. It takes that kind of specific energy and clear imaginative thought. Once I can tap into that energy I can make a list and progress but if I somehow don't have the starting point, I can't. The base or spark seems to be missing and the only time I feel at all close to it is first thing in the morning.

Also, I liked what you said to me very much, it resonated with me: "I would like you to vanish and cease to be except as the happy, busy executor of your smart updated to do list." That's it for now!

Thank You. Kellie

**

Hi, Kellie:

Congrats! That was a lot of good work punctuated by actual successes! Very nice!

We need to "do something" about "what state you need to be in" in order to get to the art making. It sounds like you couldn't make a list for that or quantify that because you knew intuitively that you wouldn't keep to your list if you weren't in "the right space" when art making appeared on your schedule. I think that the work of the next three weeks, in addition to all the good things you are already doing in terms of selling and networking and so on, is to *really work* on changing your mind about "what state you need to be in" in order to create.

I would love you to start to say and to believe, "I can flip the switch right now and get to the art making" and to really practice "flipping that switch" and moving fluidly and effortlessly from some task or other to studio work. That would be such a wonderful gain! I don't know if you can picture how exactly to try to make that happen but I hope that you can picture it and commit to trying to actually practice "flipping that switch." I hope that what I mean is clear and I hope that you will give it a try!

**

Clients regularly understand what I mean when I ask them to "flip the switch" and move instantly and effortlessly from, say, being an anxious person to being a calm person, from struggling to get to their creative work to moving there effortlessly, from fighting with the reality of the art marketplace to dealing with that reality calmly and directly. They understand what I mean: but can they do it? Sometimes! And isn't that something?

19. A MILLION WORDS WAITING

WHAT IF YOU WRITE A NOVEL AND PUT IT ASIDE AND WRITE AN-
OTHER NOVEL AND PUT IT ASIDE AND WRITE ANOTHER NOVEL AND
PUT IT ASIDE AND THEN, ANOTHER DOZEN NOVELS LATER, DECIDE
THAT IT IS TIME TO TRY TO PUBLISH? WHAT A SET-UP FOR PARAL-
YSIS YOU'VE CREATED! IT IS QUITE REGULARLY THE CASE THAT
A CREATIVE PERSON ACCUMULATES AN ENORMOUS INVENTORY
OF "PRODUCT"—MANY PAINTINGS, MANY SONGS, MANY STORIES,
MANY PHOTOGRAPHS, AND SO ON—AND THEN MUST DEAL WITH
THE OVERWHELMING TASK OF "MOVING ALL THAT INVENTORY."
HERE IS ONE SUCH STORY.

**

Dear Eric:

*Until I wrote my dissertation, I had no idea that I could re-
ally write. My dissertation director told me I was the best writer
he had read, which on the face of it can't be true. I am willing to
believe, though, that I'm among the best academic writers he'd
read, academics being so often not very good writers. However,
now I own my skill, which I've developed through reading a lot
and writing a lot.*

*For a period of about three years, I woke up in the middle
of every night and wrote secretly, keeping it from my partner.
During this time I wrote 14 novels and most of 2 others. But of
course the secret was a Big Problem. When it finally came out,
things were not good, especially when she asked to read one of
my stories and was shocked to find that it was (a) actually a novel, not just a story (which spoke to how I had been lying to her*

and also neglecting things I needed to do in favor of this writing), (b) erotic, and (c) religious. We are both religious, but the combination didn't thrill her. She read about three or four pages, I think.

She has been adamantly opposed to my publishing any of this work both because she disapproves of the content and also because it takes my attention away from what I need to be doing, which is earning money teaching college online. It's a cushy job in many ways, but I really don't like doing it anymore; however, I need to. My theory is that if I combined it with other things I want to do, publishing and more writing and publishing, etc., I would dislike it a lot less and it would take up a lot less time.

She and I are ending our 18-year relationship and becoming family rather than partners and I no longer feel bound by any constraints around this. Much of her concern had to do with my not being able to maintain privacy with this writing, even with a pseudonym, and how it would reflect on her. She truly is not as self-referential as I'm making her sound but the part about writing when I should have been living up to my money-earning responsibilities is certainly true.

I am also coming out of a 3.5-year deep depression that has pretty much immobilized me. I've been chronically depressed most of my life and have managed it, more or less, with overworking, under-sleeping, overeating, taking stimulants, smoking pot, drinking, and remaining immobilized for substantial periods of time. I've been clean and sober for 21.5 years now and I can no longer overwork. I still overeat, over- and under-sleep, and take stimulants, although now they're prescribed: Ritalin really helps me keep focus.

At the moment I'm couch surfing with my stuff in storage, having pared way down, until I move into my own place. A friend from AA and a friend from another support group are sharing the blessing (LOL) of my company three days at a time. My new place is in a rooming house where I'll share a bathroom and a *kitchen and have my own room, and I'm really looking forward to it. I'll have very little upkeep to do, I'll be able to get around on foot (I don't have a car), and I will have no obligation to be roommate-ish.*

Right now my biggest challenge, in addition to, or perhaps because of, all of the above, is that I'm not writing. I've got a lot of stories going on inside me, a whole different set from the series of 14+ I've written, and the characters are starting to come alive, but nothing on paper yet. And I really, really don't want to lose that part of my life. On the contrary, I want to expand it a lot.

My goals? I want to self-publish at least one novel—format it, get a cover made, and publish it. I want to post at least once to my two blogs: I have a mental list as long as both arms of short pieces I want to write and upload. And I want to finish the two novels that are nearly done. My "wow" goals are to begin the new series (I have two partial stories, maybe 20 pages each, to work with) and, most importantly, to get back in the swing of writing, which I used to do daily and now I haven't done for nearly a year. Maybe this should go on both lists, or maybe it's really the only goal.

Best, Dylan

**

Hi, Dylan:

Can you clarify for me a little? You say that you've written fourteen novels? Are any of them published? Are they ready for publication? If some are and some aren't, can you explain to me how many are "really done" and how much work is needed on the others? Your fourteen novels, if self-published and promoted, might actually make you money, so I want to focus my attention there for the moment and get some clarification from you about the status of those fourteen novels.

Best, Eric

**

Hi, Eric:

Well, this is what I can tell you.

Of the 14 more or less finished novels, 11 are ready for publication and 3 need some more editing, not much. I call these stories Story #1, Story #2, and so on--no titles yet, but all are part of a series.

In addition, Story #15 has about 136,000 words and needs, I think, about 5,000 more. Story #16 has about 80,000 words and needs about 40,000 to 50,000 more. I know where I'm going with both of these.

Then there are Story #17, about 16,000 words and Story #18, about 4,300 words. I like both of them; but between the time when I started them last year and now I have come to realize that they will be part of a different series. I will probably self-publish the ones in the first series, although I don't have a plan for promoting them yet, since I don't use social media in my own name and haven't started in my pseudonym.

That's where I am so far. I hope this clarifies things.

Dylan

**

Hello, Dylan:

Well, this is actually a massive undertaking. I think I would suggest that you come up with an (excellent) name for the series and (excellent) individual titles for the novels, begin thinking about (excellent) covers based on your title name and theme, and think through how you will generate interest in your series before you start self-publishing them. That is, I think it would be wise if you spent the next two weeks creating a brand idea and a marketing and promoting plan for the series. I hope you agree.

**

TWO-WEEK REPORT

Hi, Eric:

These two weeks has been eventful.

I moved into a new home, a very complicated move even though only a short distance, a result of the separation from a long-term relationship.

I had an argument with my sort-of former partner that was hurtful to both of us, and I'm still reeling from it. We haven't spoken since, so I imagine she is reeling too.

I've carried the load of 10 classes, about 300 students, until this past weekend. I have half that many classes and students now, which is a great relief.

What I haven't done is any work on preparing to publish any of the stories. I was feeling really low about that today, the sort of chronic self-criticism that's far too familiar and way too deep a groove.

But I started getting out of it today, too. I have a list as long as my arm of short non-fiction things I want to write about, and I started one today. Only about 600 words, not very good, but it was thrilling. I realized that, sure, I should be unpacking; and yes, I do have to get final grades made and submitted by midnight; but more importantly, I need to start writing again.

That's my big body-certain realization of the week.

Along with that, I decided to look at when I've done writing, how long it has been since I've done it, to see if I can get a clue to what got in the way and what's out of the way now. So I made a list of when I started and finished the various stories and their word counts, and I'm pasting it into this email. I have no idea whether it's of any interest to you, or helpful for your work, but it's helpful to me.

I think where I want to start right now in my work with you is writing again. I used to write every day without fail, and that's when I could really write. I have fewer pressures now, but still plenty of obligations to keep the limits clear, which is what I need to get work done, so I want to do it.

I hope this is of some help to you. Below is my list.

Best, Dylan

Story #1 - began 11/24/06, finished 1/14/07; final revisions 5/11/09 - 135,810 words

Story #2 - began 1/11/07, finished 10/4/09 - 78,285 words

Story #3 - began 1/30/07, finished 6/15/09 - 74,639 words

Story #4 - began 2/8/07, finished 6/28/07 - 114,566 words

Story #5 - began 4/26/07, finished 7/6/08 - 58,250 words

Story #6 - began 11/1/07, finished 1/13/08 - 82,717 words

Story #7 - began 3/9/08, finished 5/3/09, needs final revisions - 69,191 words

Story #8 - began 8/20/07, finished 7/9/08; needs final revisions - 73,025 words

Story #9 - began 12/2/07, restarted 4/18/10, finished 9/16/10 - 79,071 words

Story #10 - began 11/1/08, finished 4/27/09 - 79,282 words

Story #11 - began 7/13/08, finished 4/23/09 - 75,150 words

Story #12 - began 11/1/09, finished 12/3/10, needs final revisions - 193,477 words

Story #13 - began 10/6/09, restarted 2/12/10, finished 5/25/10, revised 4/17/12, needs final revisions - 148,203 words

Story #14 - began 3/7/10, finished 8/30/10 -118,206 words

Story #15 - began 4/28/10, as of 9/4/11 had 136,145 words, needs about another 5,000 or 6,000 words to finish

Story #16 - began 6/22/10, as of 9/7/11 had 82,314 words, needs about another 30,000 or 40,000 words to finish

Story #17 - began 7/14/10, as of 12/24/10 had 15,909 words; will probably move this to the other series and write another 100,000 words or so

Story #18 - began 4/14/11, as of 11/1/12 had 4303 words; will move this to the other series and write at least another 100,000 words or so

**

Hello, Dylan:

The need to write makes perfect sense and maybe is especially necessary as a sort of healing or grounding place during this period of emotional upheaval and busy school duties. So, yes, let's make the writing the priority and perhaps you can create a plan and schedule for yourself for the next three weeks that will allow you to pay regular, disciplined attention to some new writing.

But I would also love to get a second goal on the table, which is to begin to deal with this quite incredible backlog of unpublished "stories," as you call them. Can you create a plan for dealing with them or perhaps the first steps of such a plan? I imagine it is beyond daunting and maybe immobilizing to have so many back projects that need attention, but they *do* need attention. So that is what I would suggest for you: that you commit to the regular new writing and the beginnings of a plan to deal with the backlog.

**

Imagine yourself in Dylan's situation. You have a million words sitting there that for whatever reasons you couldn't deal with in a timely fashion. By all rights the effort to put them into

*the world should have occurred as and when they were complet-
ed. But that didn't happen. Now you want to publish. How daunt-
ed and immobilized would you feel with those million words
sitting there? What might you try to get them moving into the
world? And what odds would you give yourself that you could see
the project through? The headline: try, if you can, to publish a
finished thing before moving on to the next thing!*

20. BEAUTIFUL AFFORDABLE JEWELRY

VERY OFTEN A PERSON WHO HAS FIGURED OUT A WAY TO MAKE A MARGINAL LIVING IN THE ARTS, SAY BY PRODUCING A LOT OF CERAMICS, JEWELRY, OR STATIONERY, MUST SPEND SO MUCH TIME AND ENERGY PRODUCING "MORE PRODUCT" FOR THE NEXT CRAFT SHOW OR THE NEXT ROUND OF DISTRIBUTION THAT SHE NEVER QUITE BECOMES THE ARTIST SHE ALWAYS DREAMED OF BECOMING. HOW TO GET OFF THIS MERRY-GO-ROUND OR ROLLERCOASTER OF CONTINUAL CRAFT PRODUCTION? AND WHERE WILL YOU BE IF YOU DO MANAGE TO GET OFF, GIVEN THAT YOU WILL SUDDENLY FIND YOURSELF AT THE BEGINNING OF WHAT MAY BE ITS OWN DIFFI-CULT ADVENTURE?

**

Hi, Eric:

I am in one of the stages of healing from the most painful and challenging three-and-a-half years of my life. My partner of fifteen years walked out one night and never returned, leaving me with debts and bills all in my name. Abandonment was my is-sue and the worst kind of abandonment happened. Dealing with that would have been enough but disaster after disaster just kept on happening, so for all of this time I have been stuck in survival mode.

For the previous fifteen years our sole income came from what I made and sold. I did many, many craft shows "cranking out" beautiful affordable jewelry and had reached the point where the next step was for me to refocus energy and time on my art life. Instead, once I was able to function again it felt like I was right back at the beginning: older, more weary, broken-hearted, broken-spirited, grateful to have jewelry that sells but far from my art life, and yet again creating for survival.

This experience has shown me that a life, even a carefully planned and lived one, can fall apart in almost an instant and the repercussions of one's choices can last for a very, very long time. I feel that most of my choices before this were fear-based and though I did the best that I could in art as well as life if things had kept going in the same way I would have kept caretaking and nurturing my issues rather than my evolution.

I now truly believe that what happened with my former partner was one of my most valuable life lessons because I could no longer outrun all of the things I feared the most: abandonment, poverty, totally crippling fear, being alone in the middle of nowhere without a support system, despair, grief. You get the picture. Over time bit by bit I am learning to make more informed self-caring choices.

Growing up poor informed my beliefs about money. I never wasted money, never overspent, never had debt, and had perfect credit. In retrospect I see that I have been afraid of money and that informed my choices in all parts of my life, including my art life. Throughout this time I have continued to create, to participate in craft shows, etc. Each proactive step forward, getting back on my feet financially, seemed to be met with a larger disaster. My survival skills have kept me standing but the ground has continued to be shaky.

Since I was a child my ability to create seems to be untouched by the vagaries of life and I am grateful for that but I am eager to enter this new place of creating from a calm center and not from fear or adrenaline. Recently I had a shift in perception, I don't know why, but I am going with it. I am tired of being afraid. Do I have real reasons to be afraid? Yes, indeed, but like storms of all kinds that cause damage they pass, yes, leaving damage, but also leaving new ground for new opportunities.

A quick story. I had to go to a major city for a show and the person I was to share a hotel room with changed her mind the day before the show. My neighbor suggested the Salvation Army but that felt like poverty thinking to me. So I googled "cool places to stay for someone who can't afford much." I found a fabulous mansion in the center of a park overlooking the city, where I was greeted by a smiling face, free parking, and a very affordable price. I had to realize that I am no longer satisfied with poverty thinking. The most amazing thing is that there are places like this everywhere, both real and metaphorical. You just have to be willing to look. So here I am a lifelong "artist" just beginning to look around and finally learning to see!

After these past few years of inner work I am now in a very different place. I am reframing my thoughts and speech. I have begun using the words "I want" to begin my sentences because, though I consider myself both strong and smart, in my whole life I have never, not even once, asked myself "What do I want?" That's a very weighty thing to have carried for over 50 years. I am determined to both learn what I want and to give myself to those things to the best of my abilities.

I have "supported" myself with my craft and that is a good thing as far as it goes. I have assets that I now can begin to use differently. That is where I am at now. I have gratitude. I have intention. I have new tools to use in this new phase of my journey. I am going to be exercising my right for a rich creative practice.

One of my biggest challenges in respect to my creative life is a lifelong one. I don't have clear identifiable artistic identity. In a lifetime of being a maker, a jeweler and an artist I have only once had a cohesive body of work. It was well received but I was more inspired by the design process rather than by actually producing the work. I still remember the joy, boundless creativity and inspiration of that time. I would like to delve into this.

I am always able to create. I am blessed in that regard but it is for me a mixed blessing. I create to make money, to survive.

Artists whose artwork you can immediately identify intrigue me. I want to "interview" them, to hear about their creative journey, because I feel that I have yet to embark on my own. Cleverness and making beautiful jewelry is no longer enough. It hasn't been for years but I am ready to go forward now. I think that I have a glimmer of the next step. My favorite words these days are ruminate and ponder ...

I think that as I continue this evolution a body of work will begin to emerge naturally. Some minimum goals for now:

1. *To generate enough income that I feel "safe" and that I'm able to pay bills and the mortgage.*

2. *To take care of myself.*

3. *To explore purely for joy other mediums like watercolor and mixed media.*

4. *I want to paint clouds. Sounds so simple but I have yet to paint one.*

5. *To make progress in understanding and starting on my creative journey. This is absolutely not about revenue.*

6. *To find a way or a discipline so that I am in charge of my time and how I use it. I want to begin my day with intent and focus. I want to create a working schedule that maximizes both my creative and practical goals. I want to end my day feeling like I stayed on track and accomplished a reasonable amount of what I had intended.*

My wow goal: It would be great if I made the leap from desire, yearning, and postponing, to finding MY creative voice & giving expression to it. The best would be working towards creating very identifiable bodies of work. I think that one of the things I am looking for is inspiration so powerful that I am compelled to bring some kind of vision to life. I have low-level inspiration all the time but I am seeking something more. After rereading all of this I can see that maybe, just maybe, I can have the art life that I have dreamed of.

Meredith

**

Hello, Meredith:

You say that you are looking for a style that is identifiable and recognizable as yours. Given your new outlook on life and your wealth of experience, how might you go about "creating" or "finding" that identifiable style? What might a plan look like to "get you" to that identifiable style, one that doesn't take too much time <smile> or involve you in too much research <smile>? That is, can you "find" that style in you right now – and if so, how might you do that finding?

Best, Eric

**

Hi, Eric:

I don't think that it a style that I am seeking. Yesterday I saw two young foxes playing tag. They were so joyfully in the moment, leaping and tumbling, eyes so bright and alert. Some music reaches in and grabs me so powerfully that I cannot move and feel lyrically alive to my core. I am transported. I think where I am going with this is that I feel in some primal way I have woken up and I am moved by so much that I feel like I am seeing everything for the very first time. I want to explore ...

Meredith

**

Hi, Meredith:

Let us keep it simple, then. For the next two weeks why don't you explore, exactly as you described the exploring you want to do, with the only addition that you will commit to spending some real time each day exploring. You decide how much time is "real time" but please commit to some real devotional exploring time every day<smile>!

**

Hi, Eric:

I feel very thoughtful these days, more responsive rather than reactive. My ninety-five-year-old mother has been having a rough time and I feel has been over-medicated to the point of hallucinations. She has been in the hospital and though she was cleared medically she clearly is not better emotionally. Her anxiety has caused her to be so off balance that she is unable to function.

I mention this because in her I see someone who has lived a very unexamined life and now with too much time on her hands I think that she doesn't know what to do with the thoughts that she is having. I am strongly advocating "talk therapy " for her along with some meditation. For the first time in both of our shared lives we are finally beginning to see and hear each other. For me this is a really good thing as I feel that her acceptance and appreciation of me is a positive in my journey.

During this time one of my cats developed a virulent cancer and I had to euthanize her. The day before all this happened I went on a daylong retreat, so I was relaxed and refreshed to deal in a responsive manner with both my mom and Alice the kitty. I now feel that I have a better understanding of the importance of self-care and I will make a conscious effort to include it in my life.

My exploration has been one of calmly producing, without ANY stress, some pretty amazing pieces of jewelry. I am doing a show this weekend so that drove my creative process. So yes I have been exploring but it feels more like a relaxing walk through a familiar landscape, driven by being able to produce "salable" work for the show). However within that constraint I have pushed the envelope and am proud of what I have created. I also have scooped up quite a few "old and unfinished" pieces and finished those, again with no stress.

I am realizing yet again how skilled I am, both in creativity and production, and I am grateful. I do regret that there is an up-coming deadline that I will not meet for some prestigious shows next year but I feel that I am working at the right speed for my journey and I just didn't produce the kind of work that will get me in this very competitive show. I might relook at my images and give it a shot. I will have to be objective.

One avenue that I am actively following is returning to school. I have always regretted that my education was so frac-tured. I was able to attend two renowned universities and basi-cally was not ready or able to complete either one. So at 60 I am ready to learn in an educational setting. I can attend a nearby college absolutely for free and also audit classes at another col-lege where there is a very active creativity center with a fully equipped metal studio.

Life is not linear and I am finally beginning to create the life I have imagined for myself. I have to really stick on track with making a steady amount of money for my plan to work. I am tak-ing a free computer course this week and meeting with someone to finally open an online shop. This is still by far the most im-portant essential move for my stability. So I feel pretty positive overall. I am reframing my thoughts in a way that supports my forward momentum ...

Best, Meredith

**

Hello, Meredith:

A lot that was good went on. Congrats! I think my only real suggestion for the next three weeks is that you stay very organized, even if organization and your current reflective state don't seem to be exactly compatible. You want to get many concrete things done and they require discipline and organization, so if you can make a plan and a schedule that serves you while at the same time remaining in this productively reflective state, I think that would be ideal. There is an ongoing strategic balance to be struck between reflecting and actually doing and I hope that you take the next three weeks to continue working on how to strike that balance.

**

Is going back to school the answer for an artist in this situation? Who can say? But the desire to go back to school speaks to the serious problems that an artist faces when she has produced "product to market" for decades and now wants to become the artist she has always hoped to become. Faced with that grand opening and with new mysteries, new doubts, and new difficulties, it is understandable that she might want some traditional help in the form of more education. Will that help actually help? Only time will tell.

21. PSYCHOLOGICALLY READY TO QUERY

THE MARKETPLACE IS RATHER A MINEFIELD. THAT, HOWEVER, IS NO REASON TO AVOID IT. JUST AS IN BATTLE YOU MUST NEGOTIATE MINEFIELDS IN ORDER TO MOVE FORWARD, AS AN ARTIST YOU MUST NEGOTIATE THE CHALLENGES OF CRITICISM AND REJECTION, RUDE AND UNFAIR TREATMENT, MEAN AND NARCISSISTIC COMBATANTS, CLIQUES AND ALLIANCES, LONG MEMORIES AND SHORT MEMORIES, BOTTOM LINE REALITIES, AND EVERY OTHER MANNER OF UNPLEASANTNESS AND INJUSTICE. AND OF COURSE YOUR WORK MAY NOT BE UP TO SNUFF—THAT'S POSSIBLE, TOO! THE OCCASIONAL ARTIST FAIRS BEAUTIFULLY AND WILL REPORT THAT THE ART MARKETPLACE HAS PROVEN A HEAVEN: MOST WILL REPORT THAT IT SEEMS MUCH MORE LIKE THE OTHER PLACE.

**

Hello, Eric;

I have been writing or trying to write mystery novels since 1992 when I joined a mystery-writing group that developed out of a writing class. Others in the group are published authors, two of whom sell quite well, but I'm still unpublished.

I submitted a short story to some mystery magazines, but it was rejected although I think it's very good. I have one complete draft of a mystery novel that I wrote in the early 90's, but never sent to agents or publishers (since I didn't think it was publishable, although I like many things about it). Now I'm about to complete the first draft of another mystery novel, which I've been working on for the last few years.

In between the two more-or-less-completed novels, I have aborted some other attempts. I have never been able to write from an outline, but my problem completing writing projects is not that I digress too much – I always keep an eye on the story as a whole. The reason I give up is lack of confidence either in my writing ability or in the writing project.

Yet despite this problem, I have stuck with creative writing since it has a lot of meaning for me. I've been focused on my current novel since I was diagnosed with cancer in early 2011, and it has kept me out of depression. I'm highly motivated to finish the novel because I want to leave something behind when I die. Now it looks as if I won't die very soon, but my situation was dicier two years ago.

One of my challenges right now is to get my current writing project into publishable form. I need to keep my confidence up. I'll have a much bigger challenge when I get around to trying to sell it. I have always had a lot of trouble selling myself but that's undoubtedly more than two months away, so I won't even start the marketing process during the two-month self-coaching.

Perhaps I should also mention that I usually hate the writing process. I keep going (often slowly) because I love the product. That "wow" feeling – "I actually wrote that!" – is what motivates me to go through the painful process of writing. Anyway, the pain involved I still consider a challenge, though it's one I've gradually been mastering.

My goal for the next two months is to complete the first draft of my current writing project (probably doable in a week) and get as far as I can with the first revision. Ideally, my aim would be to complete the first revision entirely.

Miriam

**

Hi, Miriam:

As I understand it, you are a week away from finishing the draft of your current mystery? And then what is likely to happen? Do you think that you will read it, like it well enough (given that it is a draft), revise it, and then shop it around? Or do you think that you will stall in some way? If you think you might stall, what is it that would stall you? Not liking it well enough? Not wanting to finish it and then having to face the marketplace? If you suspect that you might stall, what do you think would cause the stalling?

Best, Eric

**

Hi, Eric:

Yes, I am close to finishing the first draft of my mystery novel. I even wrote a tentative climactic scene, ran it by my critique group Wednesday night, and plan to do some revision on it in the next day or two, then go on to other revisions. I need to make some changes to make the book consistent and to do a lot of cutting if possible. I'm told there are too many words for a first novel. (I now have about 110,000 words.)

After completing the revisions (which should take me at least until the end of August), I intend to try to obtain an agent for the book. What is likely to stall me, if I do in fact begin stalling, is the fear of rejection when I submit my manuscript (or even just a query letter) to agents or publishers. (I may self-publish, but believe that I should at least test the waters before doing so. Marketing will be even harder if I don't have a publisher.)

When I received only form-letter rejections for a short story I wrote, I found it very discouraging. The same thing is likely to occur with my novel, and not necessarily because it isn't any good. I know someone who had his first manuscript rejected by 40 or 50 agents before it was accepted, and he ended up selling quite well. I don't think I could keep going that long before giving up on finding an agent. Maybe one or two rejections would be enough for me to give up.

My main problem may be that I don't know if I can write something that will appeal to the general public. I am extremely introverted, sometimes painfully shy, and very much an intellectual, academic type. I'm more interested in the inner life than in "action," and I love anything abstract (philosophy, mathematics, computer programming, tax preparation, etc.), which most people don't. It's too bad I won't be marketing my book during the two-month self-coaching process, but anything you can tell me about how to go about it will be welcome.

Miriam

**

Hi, Miriam:

That's very clear. So the work for the next two weeks is finishing this draft and, if you finish it, beginning the revising process. Please do exactly that every day for a considerable amount of time every day, no matter what doubts or resistances arise. Okay?

Your second task is to completely change your mind about criticism and rejection. You must accept them both in an entirely new way. It would be criminal if you stopped submitting because of a thin skin. Published writers receive hundreds and hundreds of rejections in their lifetime. I want you to spend a little time each day over the next two weeks working with yourself to change your mind about criticism and rejection and to build a thicker skin. How you do that is for you to figure out!

**

TWO-WEEK REPORT

Eric—

First of all, I have revised my general plan. I now intend to send queries to agents before doing all the revisions on my book. I want to have ready a polished version of chapters one through three (along with some diary entries – the book will alternate diary entries and chapters) plus a polished version of the climactic scene, plus a synopsis of the book in case agents ask for any of these right away.

Then, after I research how to locate agents, and compose a query letter (with help from people I know who have gone through this process), I will send queries to a number of agents and wait to hear back from them. During the remainder of the self-coaching time, I hope to complete the synopsis of the book, finish a query letter, and at least begin making a list of appropriate agents to send it to. I doubt that I'll be ready to send queries until shortly after the self-coaching period, but I'll be psychologically ready to do it, partly due to your help.

Second, during the past two weeks I have revised my climactic scene (which I will run by my critique group on July 24), have also revised the beginning of the book (completing that on July 13), and have finished a first draft of a synopsis for the first 31 out of 39 chapters. And I'm liking the book and the way I've organized it!

Besides all that, I have made notes on most of the revisions that need to be made on the chapters in between the beginning and the ending. I have done this for chapters 4 through 31. There are only eight more chapters to plan revisions for and do a synopsis of. I have not yet planned any revisions nor done a synopsis for the 41 diary entries, which include the climactic scene mentioned above, but the diary entries will not need a lot of revision, nor will the synopsis of those be as important as that of the chapters.

Third, I have thought about how to deal with rejection. Actually, I'm not quite as thin-skinned as I made out in my last email to you (I was describing myself at my worst, which isn't right now). But I do need to work on my attitude.

One way I'm dealing with fear of rejection is the change of plan described above. Originally I was going to revise the whole book and run it by a few readers before doing more revision, and only then approach agents. I didn't tell you about wanting friends and other acquaintances to read my first revision of the book before I approached any agents – that would definitely be a kind of stalling. It would take a while and also allow for some negative responses, which would call for more revision. Even the initial revisions will take a while – I'm noticing as I read through my book that a lot of revisions are needed in the middle of it. (I'm not stalling! I really need to do these.)

Pursuing my new plan will ensure that I do my revisions fairly quickly once I get to them, and that if I don't hear from agents right away (or I receive form-letter rejections), I'll think to myself, "Good thing that I have more time to revise this book before an agent asks for the whole manuscript." (I can easily imagine agents wanting to see the whole thing because I really love this book.) If it takes a very long time to hear anything, I can always have a few people read the book while I'm waiting. This way I won't be thinking, "I screwed up on the query letter," or "Maybe these agents won't bother to reply," or other negative thoughts like, "I can't possibly sell this book because it won't interest anybody.

It really helps that I love what I've done. I am product-oriented, and when I see an end in sight, I tend to rev myself up and finish a project quickly (but not too quickly – I like what I do to be done well.) Lastly, Eric, if you have any suggestions as to what resources to use for advice on how to write query letters or how to find good lists of agents, I would certainly appreciate whatever you can tell me. I don't expect a lengthy reply (due to lack of time), but I would guess that you have some knowledge on these topics and might be able to give me a few ideas off the top of your head.

Miriam

**

Hello, Miriam:

This is excellent! It is a very sound plan and reflects your commitment to both getting the book done and standing behind it. I would suggest that you continue in exactly the same vein for the next three weeks. As to the resources you want to find, I fear that I have no specific ones to recommend but of course the Internet is full of free and often good advice on these matters, especially from romance writers, who generally do an excellent job with their synopses and query emails. I think if you do a patient Internet search you will find a lot of advice, probably a good bit of it contradictory <smile>. Please continue what you are doing!

**

It is revealing when a person announces or admits that she might stop dealing with the marketplace after one or two rejections. Even if she quickly recants and acknowledges that a ton of criticism and rejection are likely part of the process, that first admission is still telling. Will a particularly dismissive rejection undo her? Will a rejection from an agent or an editor she had her heart set on cost her a year of pain and paralysis? Let's hope not! A wise artist who knows that she is vulnerable to criticism and rejection had better be prepared to quickly heal her wounds and immediately return to the fray!

22. WHAT DO I WANT TO PAINT?

You would think that an artist would know what she wants to create and then perhaps only have difficulties with the execution. But in reality many writers do not know what they want to write, many composers do not know what they want to compose, and many painters do not know what they want to paint. This "not knowing" is really a complex of problems having to do with doubts about talent, a too-noisy mind that prevents ideas from bubbling up, a hyper-critical nature, and difficulties in discerning what their art is "really supposed to about."

**

Hello, Eric

I am a painter, specializing in portraits and the nude figure. I have been earning my living at it for seven years now, but not earning a great deal, mainly I think because of my lack of confidence and lack of business acumen.

I am 50 years old, I brought up three daughters alone who are all grown and I live alone now. I am not an organized or confident person but somehow I have managed to find venues to do live sketching and to show my work in order to procure commissions, sometimes in coffee shops on a regular basis or galleries and even for a year in a London undercover market. I have also done some teaching and the running of local art groups, which I enjoy but don't want to do too many as they take up valuable painting time.

My portrait commissions were always very stressful to me, but my customers were always very happy. I have done many craft fairs and events where I have sketched people in half an hour on the spot, which has always been a great crowd puller.

I always did my portraits in pastel but am not enjoying my results any more. A year and a half ago I sold my house and was able to manage without worrying about money for a while and during that time I followed my intuition and started doing nude sketches in pen and ink. They are getting very good reviews and I am a member of The Guild of Erotic Artists and sometimes exhibit with them in London, and I also show them at fetish markets, and I want to do commissions in that style too. But the cost of it all is creeping in and making it harder to show them. I have lost my confidence at getting venues and doing my commissions and completely lost confidence in doing my live sketches.

When things got serious money-wise a couple of months ago I started selling on eBay, and although I am selling regularly now, it is not enough. But I am building up a following and people all over the world are buying my originals and giving me amazing feedback So I am feeling better because of that but I need to be more prolific. I am also hoping to keep a regular monthly slot at a fetish market.

My creative challenges are therefore to become more prolific and organized. I struggle to just make a decision of what to work on and just get on with it. When I finally feel I can paint I can't decide what to paint and my mind gives me too any options so I want to explode. I've read about it in your books, but still I struggle to make those decisions, it feels like I am always waiting for someone else to tell me what to do (a legacy from mother and ex-husband, I know, but still it snookers me every time).

I want to feel content to fill my day with painting and I want to learn to switch my phone off and not respond to all the people that seem to wants a piece of me. I respond to everyone like a robot; I feel I am supposed to just be on call all the time. I also want to be braver to paint more of the types of expressive paintings I enjoy rather than labored detailed pictures, although *my mind tells me I'm not a proper artist if I don't labor for hours getting technique right.*

I am disorganized and I long to be organized, because then maybe my head won't want to explode all the time when I try to plan what to do next. So I guess my biggest challenges are doing the kind of paintings that will bring in enough to then pay for the exhibiting and promotion of the new work I'm doing. And I really believe that if I can become prolific enough I could do that, but I procrastinate and lose confidence and end up producing nothing some days.

I don't want a part-time job. I've tried that and I then have no energy for my art and all my family commitments. I just need to paint all day. My minimal goals would be to become more prolific, set goals and learn to write lists that don't frighten me, to not become so reclusive when I'm in painting mode, and to just sketch and paint for the joy as well as for money. And maybe I should have a working day, certain hours that I religiously stick to and honor and to not put everyone else first.

Long-term goals would be to become so good at live sketching that I don't get paralyzed with fear and then not offer it at a venue when it can be such a good earner. All that would take is regular live sketching to improve. I also wish to be able to market my new erotic series and sell charcoal portraits of famous people through eBay and my website, plus all the pictures that I get inspired to do myself.

I want my confidence back.

Brenda

**

Hello, Brenda:

I am going to take you at your word <smile> and agree with you that getting much better organized will allow you to both become more prolific and feel more confident. So, what exactly would that organization look like? Please describe in careful, concrete terms how you want to spend your day: how many hours on which kind of work, how many hours on which other kind of work, how many hours on art marketing, and so on. Please create a detailed weekly schedule and let's see what that looks like.

Second, please describe to me what you are going to try to do to "make choosing easier"? See if you can put into words your plan for "strong choosing" or "easy choosing" or however you think you want to say that <smile>. So, let's see what your new weekly schedule and your new plan for choosing look like!

Best, Eric

**

Hi Eric,

I think my ideal weekly schedule would look like this:

Rise at 6 am on weekdays, have coffee and do my reading for half an hour to an hour, then maybe a short meditation. Switch my phone off at 7 am. Switch computer on, update Facebook and website blog without getting hooked into chatting to anybody online. Start painting at 7.30am work until at least 1 or two although maybe longer if I have no other plans or commitments.

Every day of the week I would like to have listed a small cleaning job around the house to do so I don't have to do a big clean up and so it doesn't seem so daunting just to do one small job regularly. A nap if I'm tired and still at home in the afternoon, because I would like to have the energy to do a bit of art in the evening sometimes. Evenings can be for uploading and dealing with eBay sales, and pen and ink sketches and maybe any research that's creatively related.

When I drive to visit my family I try and pack everybody in on one day but it never works, I just seem to be rushing around all day, so I need to work out how often to see them all. Weekend kept for pleasure and relaxation unless I'm feeling creative and really want to keep painting. I would also like to do my food shopping regularly and even eat at regular times.

It all looks so easy when it's written down.

As for choosing, I sometimes get so confused about what I want to paint or what I should paint, that I feel overwhelmed and depressed, it's as though when I choose to do a charcoal portrait for instance, then all the other options, pen and wash nudes, bright colorful acrylics, experimenting with oils and watercolor, all come rushing into my head demanding that I'm missing an opportunity to do them. Often I get so confused that I do nothing and then I hate myself.

So I guess the answer comes back to lists of things I want to do and then putting each thing into a calendar so that the decision is made for me ahead of time and when I wake up I should just do whatever is on my list without question!! I keep wanting to create this list but the fear is so great.

A strong choice could be something that I would be able to put on eBay to sell, or maybe even it could be something that stretches me like a watercolor. I'm not even sure what a strong choice should be for me. An easy choice could also be to churn something out to sell on eBay, or it could be playing with watercolor knowing I'm experimenting so I'm not expecting it to be perfect!!!! Oh my Lord I'm getting a headache thinking about it!!!!!!!!!!!!

Sorry Eric.

The need to earn money makes it feel like a strong choice from that perspective, but not necessarily from a creative perspective!!

Help!!!

Brenda

**

Hi, Brenda:

Yes, it feels daunting <smile>. Let's consider the work of the next two weeks the following. You will keep to your new schedule, commit to some piece of work and do it (and if you finish it, commit to the next piece and do it), and try to work out "on the side" what are the right creative choices for you at the moment. While you are figuring that out, however, you must make art! So those are three tasks: keep to the schedule, commit to and make art, and think through your overall plan about making art.

**

TWO-WEEK REPORT

Hi Eric,

I'm trying not to be too angry with myself but my two weeks hasn't been as disciplined and prolific as I see in my imagination. I recognize what I'm doing, I'm dancing to the tune of everyone else, answering phone calls to friends who want to talk for hours, feeling guilty about not seeing enough of my children and family members, not having the assertiveness to tell my man that I need my work space when he's here. I almost do it subconsciously, it's like a reflex action, I was brought up to do as I'm told and when anyone is a little more assertive than me, even politely, I just re-act and put them first.

I keep responding to everyone else and then realize that another day has gone by when I haven't done much creative work, either for my soul or my income, my money situation is such that I need to be working all day to produce work to sell or I could soon be in deep trouble, yet my conditioning of "being there" for everyone else seems stronger and more automatic than putting my career first. The realty is I don't let people know how badly I have to paint because I am ashamed that I'm not making enough money and they'll just tell me to get a job.

I know assertiveness is the first key. I've just ignored a call whilst writing this and feel very rude not to have answered it and yet strangely relieved not to be at the beck and call of someone else. The second key is the self-discipline to set a schedule and paint for the required amount of hours. But maybe the main is deciding what to draw. I get very muddled, but I am trying to narrow it down.

I seem to be an extremist in everything I do, when I do ignore people and try to work, I then become reclusive and don't want to see anyone. I don't know how to find a middle ground.

Today I am alone. I got up late because I'm tired after being with people and am trying to decide whether to tidy the house in order to make room for creativity or to just paint amid the disorder. I'm also unsure what I want to paint.

Then comes the feeling of overwhelm! Then depression sets in, then I'm angry at myself and want to avoid everyone because of the feeling of shame that now I'm finally on my own and I'm not doing anything,

Sorry this sounds negative, I just need to break this spiral I'm in.

Kind regards

Brenda

**

Hi, Brenda:

There is no way to break an old habit except by really trying to break it. You have three new habits to put into place, as I see it: to start the day with your creative work and nothing else, even if you don't know what to draw or paint; to refuse any longer to use your usual ways of distracting yourself; and to be assertive in making real time and space for your creative efforts.

If you don't institute these habits no one else will for you. There may be "underlying issues" that affect your desire to do the art but for the moment—the next three weeks, say—I think your best bet is to demand of yourself that you practice these three habits every day, intentionally and seriously.

**

Thank you Eric. I have written out the three habits I need to break, I am going to commit to a report of sorts every day that I am going to send to you but will write NO REPLY NEEDED at the top. It is purely for me to make a commitment to actually look at how I function each day. I'm not expecting them to be read, it is just a way of me reporting to myself about what I am achieving each day. I've tried diaries and I always give up. But if I send a report to you I will feel more compelled to follow through.

I PROMISE I will not do this forever. It is just to get me started . Maybe for one week, then Ill try a diary again.

Kindest regards, Brenda

**

Yesterday I watched myself and I watched myself this morning too. How easily I respond to everyone without even realizing I am being distracted from my purpose. But I did refuse to go out last night because I desperately needed sleep in order to work today, and this morning I have already been distracted by phone calls. But it is now 11 am and I am now about to focus. Phone on silent (I haven't found the audacity to switch it off yet but I hope that will come next).

Sending an email every day to report feels important.

Brenda

**

Hi Eric,

I feel I am letting myself down badly, I'm letting distractions get in the way, I worry that a depression is masking any desire to really create. It's as if there is no point. I cant find the joy of doing. It feels lonely and pointless. But I know that I just have to keep trying every day. So I guess that's what I'll do.

Kind regards. Brenda

**

Hello, Brenda:

There is the art and there is life. Work on both and affirm both. Work to reduce the sadness and the emotional distress by changing your life however you need to change it. At the same time, work on the art and make it one of your meaning opportunities. You must make meaning and you must change your life. You probably have a lot to do and not much spirit or energy with which to do it and yet only you can do it.

Best, Eric

**

When we need to make many changes, and when what prevents us from making those changes are chronic sadness, life-long habits, profound meaning issues, and our formed personality, how can we begin? We have little energy for beginning; we see little point in beginning; we are already disappointed in our efforts at change before we begin. We predict more failure and an even deeper sadness. So, how can we begin? By flipping the switch that exists somewhere in our being, the switch that clears the cobwebs and releases the past, and standing up straight on some brand new day. Find that switch; embrace that metaphor!

23. PERVASIVE DISCOURAGEMENT

"I SHOULD HAVE DONE MORE. I SHOULD HAVE HAD BETTER LUCK. I SHOULD HAVE BEEN ACKNOWLEDGED BY NOW. I SHOULD HAVE SOLD BETTER AND HAD MORE SUCCESSES. I SHOULD HAVE SHOWN MORE COURAGE, MORE DISCIPLINE, MORE DEVOTION, MORE GUTS. I SHOULD HAVE PAID MORE ATTENTION, MADE MORE CONNECTIONS, LEARNED MY CRAFT BETTER, NOT GOTTEN SO DEFLECTED AND DIS-TRACTED. NOW I AM COMPLETELY DISCOURAGED. I AM SO DEEPLY DISCOURAGED THAT MY IDEAS BORE ME AND I HAVE NO MOTIVA-TION WHATSOEVER. I AM REALLY QUITE DONE FOR." HOW MANY ARTISTS ARE THINKING THIS, SAYING THIS, AND FEELING THIS? MAYBE THE MAJORITY ...

**

Hello, Eric:

I primarily lean toward writing, though my academic back-ground is in theatre arts. Initially, I had planned to major in En-glish in college -- during my high school years the only thing I really excelled in was writing, particularly fiction and poetry. During my sophomore year in college I took an introduction to theatre and an intro to film class. At the same time I realized I wasn't going to resonate with the instructors who taught the gateway literature courses that were prerequisites to the cre-ative writing classes I was really interested in, but terrified of, so I gravitated to theatre, and never took a creative writing class at all.

I dropped the idea of an English major in favor of the much "cooler" (and actually much more "holistic" – a theme in my life) offerings of the theatre department. I graduated with a costume design emphasis, though I really had much broader interests than just costuming. I'd sung throughout high school and earlier, and loved musical theatre, but my theatre training taught me, early on, that acting wasn't for me... having to think about blocking as well as my lines was too exhausting and confounding, and I was profoundly inhibited and shy.

I "might" have been interested in directing or playwriting, but never allowed myself to admit that. I'd have had to put myself too much on the line, and I would have had to interact with others too assertively, which I was just not socially developed enough to do. The music department in my little Calvinist, Christian, fundamentalist school was ALL religiously oriented, which was just not my thing, so I never once considered majoring in voice, though I had a voice that was really fairly operatic – (too bad; The Met missed out on that one).

I also took art classes throughout my high school and college years, but I never realized there might be a possibility of making a living as an artist, so I sort of avoided the idea of pursuing visual arts as anything other than just a hobby, though truthfully I was—and AM—quite drawn to making art. When I realized it was going to be a hard-go to make a living in theatre, and that my undergraduate training was really only preparing me to pursue an MFA—which I couldn't afford, especially if the outcome of the MFA was going to be an "iffy" job at best, this understanding having been constantly drilled into us, I just set aside the idea of doing anything serious with any of my creative interests.

I eventually got a masters of arts in teaching – never got a teaching job after that and ended up working in a bank for 7 years – but during the time I was working on the MAT, I needed to take some English classes to fill out endorsement requirements, and I opted to take a creative writing class at the local community college. My instructor wondered out loud why I and another student, "the two best writers in the class," were so humble about our work. For me, it wasn't really "humility" so much as just discouragement – the belief that I didn't have it in me for an uphill battle, which I'd been told countless times it was always going to be, even for "good" writers, so why invest myself, and why spend the time?

Since then, as a "hobby," I've written a little poetry, taken some workshops ... this has been a consistent interest, but I don't do that much with it. I berate myself that I don't have books upon books of poetry, and that I haven't been widely published by now, but I don't and I haven't (though of the seven poems I've actually submitted over the course of my lifetime only two have not been published).

I just don't force myself to write and write. I brown out, instead. I've gone through several phases of being interested in screenwriting, and have, during those phases, studied, studied, studied screenwriting (taking a couple of screenwriting workshops, too, where the instructors were, as they had been in my theatre classes during my undergraduate schooling, messengers of doom right from the onset, so why bother...) I've tried to separate the doom and gloom "reality" from the actual process of getting a story out onto a page, but I've never been quite able to get past the "why bother" stage when I hit a wall (which is usually within the first 5 or so pages). Yet this interest still rears its head.

My interests: Still, at this point, poetry, screenwriting, but fiction, too, now. I mentioned I'd started working on a little Twitter novel, but that's really more of a poem, with 140-word verses ... I wanted to see what that was going to be like to write with the 140 word-to-a-scene restriction, and it turns out it's sort of interesting. It's sort of a poem, sort of a short story, with the scene-to-scene storyboard images of a screenplay. At this stage of my life I'm also interested in memoir, creative nonfiction, patching together my experiences into a cohesive whole. And recently I've become interested in graphic novels, and have an idea I'd like to pursue along those lines, too.

My biggest challenges are:

1. *Pervasive discouragement.*

2. *Braking on my ideas because "why bother?"*

3. *"Browning out" when I hit a wall.*

4. *Going in another direction when I hit a wall, and dropping what I've already done.*

5. *Distracting myself, telling myself other things (anything else) are more important to be doing at this particular moment in time/space.*

6. *Blanking.*

7. *Frustration.*

8. *Overwhelming myself.*

9. *A sense of needing to protect myself and my creation from being decimated by criticism (not so much this, anymore, but it's still there, a little, I think).*

10. *Worrying that I should be spending my time "being productive," organizing my house, taking care of business, doing "important stuff," etc., etc., etc., and guilting myself into stopping.*

11. *Skipping out on doing my creative projects because I actually AM being productive in my day-to day-work and then losing momentum and dropping the project.*

Minimum goals:

1. *Write for an hour a day, at least 5 days a week and sticking with it:*

2. *Continue to work on my Twitter novel. I can write 3 – 4 pages in an hour a day if I don't blank or ditz out. I*

have no idea where it will take me, no outline. I'm following the characters and letting the process of doing it take me to the next step. I'm also experimenting with the structure. I *might* want to try to publish it, but not necessarily on Twitter.

3. *Keep notes on ideas for, and outline, a number of creative nonfiction pieces that keep coming up for me right now. Work on putting some of these ideas together into an essay or two. Finish the essay I started a couple of weeks ago, and let that lead me to the next step (Day 6 and 7?).*

Wow! that would be great goals:

1. *Finish basic Twitter novel --*

2. *Take notes on and do a draft of a poem a week. Maybe not a finished piece – unlike prose, I have no problem finishing poems; sometimes they have to mull awhile. By the end of two months, I'll have a collection to work and re-work, and with which to move forward into the fall and the winter. Maybe write on a theme. Basically, I want to get in the habit of being able to move from one thing to another without losing the one I'm not working on right at the moment.*

3. *Get the breezeway cleared out, painted and set up as a studio of sorts before the end of July, so I might still have some warm weather in which to work out there.*

It this too scattered? Too lightweight? Too much? Unrealistic? I'm looking to be able to manage this with my work schedule, which is lighter right now, but may not be come August.

Gabriela

**

Hi, Gabriela:

This is very clear <smile>. I would make the following suggestion. Yes, screenplays are extremely hard to sell and so are probably to be avoided. But novels aren't impossible to sell, because, first of all, publishers still do want them and, second of all, you can always self-publish. So I suggest that you work on your novel – but as a "real" novel not bound or confined by some artificial device like Twitter.

You are asking, after all, to be freer, to not be "lightweight" <smile>, and to do something that maintains your interest in the face of disappointments and discouragement. A "real" novel (as opposed to a Twitter novel), one that is rich and meaningful to you, might do all of that. That might be the project to work on an hour a day, five days a week. Thoughts?

Best, Eric

**

Hi, Eric!

What attracts me and sort of excites me about the "Twitter novel" idea IS the format. The fact that is has to be concise, and tight scene to scene like a storyboard. One of the things I have difficulty with when I write is fuzzing out when I have to keep on going and going.

At this point this seems to be working for me better than regular fiction, which I tend to peter out with. Here, it's "what's next, what's next, what's next," it's more immediate, and it's sort of livelier than what I normally come up with. Yes, it is an artificial device, but a lot of poetry, which I'm more comfortable with, is also structural like this. I guess I've been looking at it as an epic poem morphed into fiction.

As I've gotten a little farther into it I'm realizing that I'm getting some direction and am formulating characters... and as they all get underway, I may end up needing to drop the 140 character bit and just run with it, but for right now it seems to be okay. I'm comfortable with it. The nice thing is that if and when I get around to dropping the 140-character format, I can fill it in and still not lose the structure of the story.

For me, right now, my main concern is getting the images out of my head and onto the page and maintaining momentum. Historically that's been my downfall. And I'm afraid I'll lose momentum and the immediacy if I drop the 140-character restriction.. It'll have to be re-written at some point, anyway, in a normal format. This is the skeleton and it's more just like a trick to keep me going, "what's next, what's next."

Ok, so the novel it is, then. I wrote yesterday, did not today. I've been trying to do my writing in the morning before I leave the house, so I'd better sign off right now (now that the 5th of July fireworks revelers have retired, thankfully), so I can get tomorrow's hour in before I have to get to work.

Thanks, Eric!

Gabriela

**

Okay, Gabriela:

Then we have a plan for the next two weeks: the novel, whether Twitter-y or whether it spills over those banks! And it would be nice if you also committed to some daily amount of time – one hour, two hours – as part of this deal, but that is up to you <smile>!

**

TWO-WEEK REPORT

This is what happened: I wrote one hour a day for the first five days on "The Novel," two days on, two days off, three days on. I abandoned the "Twitter" restriction fairly quickly, and was writing in long paragraphs. But I got (increasingly) REALLY, RE-

ALLY bored with it, even though I was sort of proud of myself for moving forward, sort of changing perspective when I thought it was called for, fleshing out characters.

I didn't like these characters, though, and I didn't like the story. I had second thoughts about an African-American character, a 16-year-old girl, telling myself it was presumptuous to add her as a prominent character, even though I know I can write fairly knowledgeably about young persons of another race.

The story itself was clear, ok prose, I guess. There was some energy, but I lost steam, one line into my 13th page (so, all told, with the three pages I'd already written, I wrote about a little less than two pages a day). THEN as the steam was dissipating, I got hit over the head with an inspiration to write a poem, so before I lost the idea, I wrote that for an hour for the next two days, directly after the last three novel days. THEN I felt guilty and discouraged for abandoning the novel.

Then I got sort of aggravated with the whole thing and stopped writing altogether for the entirety of last week, while I "thought about" writing an essay I really DO want to write, but couldn't "seem to find the time" for last week. I didn't get a chance to write yesterday. Once again stymied, balking, resistant and spinning my wheels.

When I get like this it is as if I'm a three-year-old refusing to do something I'm being forced to do, sort of a tantrum-reaction. Or an intransigent teenager. And the feeling IS one of boredom, and sort of flipping the channel - like a feeling of "don't make me sit through this ... I'll die of boredom!" so I just walk out of the room. I thought a lot about it, but couldn't really coach myself out of it. When I stop like this, it's a deep resistance.

I will finish the poem, and have another on the way, too. But I almost always finish the poems I start. Faster final product, and not boring. So that's where I'm at right now. I won't get a chance to write today, so I'll have to pick up on ... whatever ... tomorrow.

Gabriela

**

Hello, Gabriela:

"Boredom" in this context is likely a meaning problem <smile>, one that translates as "this writing probably doesn't matter all that much, either to me or to anyone else." I wonder if you can come at the "writing issue" from the perspective of making some decisions about "what sort of writing would indeed matter," hopefully landing on some meaningful themes, principles, values, subjects, or however to put it, choosing "the prospectively most meaningful" one, and committing to it for a real period of time, come hell or high water and even come boredom? That would be my suggestion to you.

**

The goal of traditional therapy is insight. The goal of existential therapy is renewed hope. Many artists arrive at a hopeless place and need, in addition to whatever else they may need, a renewed sense of hope. How is that renewal possible after a lifetime of disappointments and too much painful reality? It is possible because "the past does not predict the future" and "today is the first day of the rest of your life." The future just might be different! And today is the day to influence its direction. If you can settle into that understanding, hope might return.

24. JUST PLOUGH ON REGARDLESS

SHOWING UP. PLOUGHING ON. DOING THE WORK DIRECTLY IN FRONT YOU. CONTINUING. STAYING PUT. PERSPIRING. WORKING. NOT LEAVING. THERE IS A CORE LEARNING THAT EVERY CREATIVE PERSON NEEDS TO TAKE IN AND APPLY TO HIS OR HER CREATIVE LIFE: THE WORK ONLY GETS DONE IF YOU DO IT. PAINTINGS, SYMPHONIES, AND NOVELS ARE JUST LIKE LOAVES OF BREAD AND SKYSCRAPERS: THEY MUST BE MADE. HOW ODD TO IMAGINE OTHERWISE! AND YET COUNTLESS ARTISTS AND WOULD-BE ARTISTS ARE WAITING FOR THEIR DOUGH TO RISE, SOMEHOW HAVING FORGOTTEN ALL ABOUT THE KNEADING.

**

Hello, Eric:

After working as a mental health nurse and research assistant from 1980-1995, I decided to stay home with my young family for a couple of years. This was a great time full of play parks and picnics and playdough and paint, as well as lots of music and books and Disney movies, and I feel that my children have benefitted from that time as they are pretty happy and blossoming (I think! - yes, they are).

Recognizing that I had suppressed somewhat my own creative instincts (possibly due to a culture of self-denial here in my home country) but also in order to participate in what at that time was quite a serious and frankly pessimistic version of psychiatry, I suddenly felt inclined to pursue some more creative activities and ideas. At the same time I furthered my studies in psychology at night school and entered university as a mature full-time student, becoming fascinated by social anthropology and ethnographic methods of research.

During fieldwork for my PhD I came across art as therapy (art classes, rather than art therapy sessions) and after I wrote my thesis and passed the viva committee, a sudden burst of inspiration produced a novel and several pieces of poetry and short stories (a few published). With all my children in school I recommenced work in the health service in 2005 but became ill with an inflammatory lung disease and was put out of work in 2007.

I re-wrote the novel while convalescing, then (foolishly) took a full time post as a research assistant in a university department (not my alma mater). That job was extremely demanding but I coped well for a year and produced a well-received report. However, my youngest child was not coping well with the long hours I was working and I put forward my case for a more respectful workload. It was a temporary position, however, and the threat of termination of contract was held over me. Also, I had been replacing two lecturers who were on maternity leave for a year. When they came back I received severe treatment and criticism from them (never been criticized in work before as always worked well and conscientiously and had a spotless reputation among colleagues in all disciplines).

I became ill again with both the respiratory illness and what amounted to an anxious and depressed state. My GP persuaded me to leave and after six months on antidepressants I got myself off them and wrote a creative journal, exercised, spent time with my family, and generally restored my health and well-being. That was three years ago. Currently I am completing a book based on my research findings and tying it in with current debates on creative mental health. Once that is completed I am dying to re-write the novel again as I have a sense of the whole thing now that I want to get down.

My problem is that I keep letting myself be drawn into situations where my time and energy are usurped and I then use it as an excuse to shelve my own creative work. At the same time, I have had some very good feedback on it from literary people and I feel that not only would it be attractive to a publisher but that I have an emotional need to finish and release it - except that I feel inadequate to the task of dealing with any possible success or perhaps negative attention that might come with its publication.

On the one hand, I am comfortable discussing issues with people of various backgrounds and enjoy constructive debate. On the other hand, though, I have had experiences of 'freezing' or going blank in front of an audience while lecturing/tutoring (which I did part-time for a while as well). This thought puts me off approaching literary events. Finally, when I get going on something creative, the motivation and momentum are there until I get near to the end of the project, then some sort of nausea takes over (not really panic, more a kind of desolation), that holds me back from taking that final leap. It is quite a stumbling block.

My goals: I would like to get the academic book out of my hair, then plough into the novel, revise it in light of the vision I have for it, then seek an agent and publisher. I am guessing at a few months for the novel, then probably a few more months of doing the rounds with agents/publishers/literary events. Secondly, the academic book will need some marketing as well and I have built up some platforms through social networking as well as past work colleagues and organizations. What concerns me again is freezing in the middle of something like a presentation or meeting. If I am booked into something I will ruminate over it for weeks and it distracts me from focusing on anything else properly and I will live in a continuous state of dread until the event is over.

My overall goal is to be a successful author, I do have a string of ideas and notes for future projects, but right now my big Wow would be to get the novel published. In the long term I would like to make enough money to live on as well as follow my goal to set up a foundation for creative support for mental health, especially for young people as I agree with the philosophy of Ivor Browne et al in Ireland that young people should be kept off medication if at all possible and supported to develop their creativity, skills and independence.

So it's really a combination: I want to be personally successful (and even feel sick saying that!), I want to allow my own creativity to develop and I want to foster it in others for their mental health and wellbeing. Hope I haven't rambled too much.

Thanks, Melanie

**

Hi, Melanie:

Thank you for this. I have a few questions.

1. Do you need the writing to earn a living? Or do you have a source of income separate from the writing that will allow you to live?

2. What is standing in the way of finishing up the nonfiction book? Is it the fear of representing it and promoting it, a lack of motivation, or are there also technical, organizational, or logical problems that need addressing before it can be finished? Can you paint me a picture of what's needed to get that book done – so that we can get on to the novel!

Best, Eric

**

Hello, Eric:

Thank you for your further message.

Firstly, apologies for the late response, but I hope it is good news that I have been tied up with much writing and wanted to get a certain amount done before sitting down to think about my answers to your questions. Once I read your response and started to think about 'painting the picture', there was a sudden release of energy and I knew exactly what to do next. I am now halfway through the final chapter of the current book and a few more days will do it, then edit and tighten up the references, then aiming at submission of the manuscript to the editor by Friday 11th July. So thank you wholeheartedly for that jolt of therapy!

Yes, there is a fear of representing the material, as it is on the one hand a bit contentious but hopefully overall constructive. I have remembered the maxim 'face the fear and do it anyway' and have decided to have the courage of my convictions. That said, the publisher is an academic house yet I am not interested in being drawn into the academic world of conferences, etc., as I have formed the opinion that more effective work is done at a more informal level and on the ground. Perhaps I should be more open-minded on that? My long-term aim with this book is to connect with a community and maybe even set up a local initiative and/or a foundation for creative mental health recovery.

This brings me to your question about making a living. Since losing my last job through an illness (I recovered well and manage my health well through being able to pace and balance my work, self-care and personal responsibilities) I have a very small income from a health service pension. It is small because I was part-time for the last six months of the health service job and because I broke service during the time my children were young; and also because I went to university as a full-time mature student for several years. My husband is self-employed and works all hours to pay the bills, so after that ramble the short answer is, Yes, I do need to earn a living from my writing. That I see as the next step - to finish the novel and get an agent.

Now in this positive state of having made a final assault on the summit of the academic book, that all sounds fine. Already however I am ruminating on what to do if the academics come calling (they may not!) and I get embroiled in that world of research, etc. It is not at this moment where I want to work and I know from past experience that it will knock out my other activities. It might be asked then, why publish the book? It is based on work I have done and an agent I know has advised me to get it out, as anything that establishes you as a published author is worth doing. It is also important work I think. It resonates with current debates in mental health care and support and as I said it is part of a long-term plan to contribute to mental health promotion, a way of giving back in the long run.

In short, I feel the academic book needs to go out and my long-term goal of mental health promotion will be supported by it. However my main drive here and now is towards creative writing in the literary fiction genre which I hope would be a commercially successful venture as well as an emotionally satisfying one, and is one that I could cope with and manage at my own pace. I hope that answers the questions sufficiently

Best wishes, Melanie

**

Hello, Melanie:

Good. Then we have a very clear goal for the next two weeks: finishing the book (with as little self-pestering, self-doubting or worries about its reception as possible!).

**

TWO-WEEK REPORT

Hello Eric,

Thanks for your message and helpful advice. I am making progress with the final sections of the academic book, thank you. Not as fast as I had hoped but moving towards the endpoint, which I do have in sight, and steadily working on a daily basis. This is the first time in a long time that I have been able to accomplish such a steady work pattern, and I think there are several reasons:

> *+ Even the very awareness of not 'self-pestering' seems to create an alert when you are doing it so you stop right away.*

+ I distracted myself from negative thoughts and future preoccupations by focusing on the task in hand and saying 'this matters.'

+ The more I did this, the easier it became, the whole knot seemed to unravel and I could see each step as a doable task, one by one.

+ Funnily enough, everything seems to have slowed down, yet at the same time I am getting more done.

+ There was a day when I was very tired and had difficulty concentrating. I focused on domestic tasks, spent some time with my family enjoying the (rare) good weather and was able to start afresh the next day, more productively.

An old adage came into my head as well that my Dad used to say and which I had not thought of in ages. 'Just plough on regardless,' he would say if you were being pulled down by something. It pops into my head now on a regular basis!

It will take me longer than the original two weeks planned to finish this book; the deadline is end of July so just over a week more should do it. Then I have plans to do stuff with my daughter so I am going to take a vacation for that second week. However, I have been reading over bits for the novel, briefly, in the evenings, just informally gathering it all together to launch into it as my next project. But I am cringing at the old drafts and think it needs to be re-written and changed quite a bit. That's for later.

To round off this stint, it was a challenge to find my own answers and solutions (with a bit of prompting and priming - thanks) but it always came through eventually and I feel stronger! For example, on that day I thought the book I'm writing was terrible, I mean pure rubbish - I was almost panicking! But I remembered that the main thing is to do the work and that helped me to plough on. Another thing then sprung to mind: the insight that the resistance and turbulence are at their worst when you are close to the breakthrough, so if you keep going resistance will at some point evaporate.

I am learning to 'trust the soup.' I'm been forever making notes and rough drafts and getting bogged down in them but I have now found that if I just get myself to the keyboard, the rest takes care of itself. The other tip I am using successfully is from one of your books: to stay focused on the purpose and even more so to 'focus on meaning rather than mood.' This is a very powerful lesson, if you're prepared to take it on.

So, that's it for these two weeks. Thanks again, Eric

All the best, Melanie

**

Hello, Melanie:

Great! That was a lot of learning and a lot of break-throughs. The two main tasks are, of course, finishing the academic book and returning to the novel. Each is in a "different place" and comes with its own challenges. Stay focused on finishing the academic book, however long it takes, and when it is really done clear your head and turn to the novel with fresh eyes, just as you are already doing. The tasks are clear and they WILL come with challenges, so use your new insights and "plough on"!

**

Very often there is a substantial project between an artist and his or her "real" project. She would love to work on her novel but she has a nonfiction book under contract and deadline. She would love to work on her large painting but her greeting card line pays the bills. She would love to create a performance piece but she has to learn a new monologue for auditions. Isn't our real work hard enough without other necessary work standing in the way? Yes, indeed; and still the only answer is to do both. There is no other answer.

25. PERFECT BLANK CANVASES

WORKING ARTISTS MAY SPEND A LIFETIME DOING COMMENDABLE WORK, WORK THAT OTHERS PRAISE AND PURCHASE, AND STILL COME UP AGAINST THE RECURRING FEELING THAT THEY HAVEN'T DONE THEIR "REAL WORK" OR THEIR "BEST WORK" YET. IS THAT RATHER MORE A MENTAL MISTAKE OR AN OBJECTIVE OPINION? PROBABLY IT IS BOTH. QUITE LIKELY WE DO HAVE GREAT WORK IN US THAT WE HAVE FAILED TO MANIFEST AND NEVER WILL BRING INTO THE WORLD. AND QUITE LIKELY WE ARE ALSO THINKING WRONG, MEASURING OUR WORK AGAINST SOME UNREAL AND IMPLAUSIBLE IDEAL OF PERFECTION. WHAT TORTURE! WE AREN'T AS GREAT AS WE MIGHT HAVE BEEN; AND WE CAN'T TRANSCEND OUR MEDIUM.

**

Dear Eric,

I spent a lot of time as a child by myself, having been born without feet, I did not have many playmates. It wasn't really a disability because I could walk, run, ride a bike, roller skate, jump rope, etc., anything the other kids could do. I just looked different and many kids would run away from me when they saw me.

I turned to drawing things from my imagination and from photos. Mostly faces or figures of people I saw in magazines, flowers, butterflies or animals. Anything pretty that I could find a picture of. It seemed to be the only thing I was interested in. Many times in school I would get in trouble by drawing instead of paying attention to the teacher.

By the time I got to high school I was selling realistic pencil portraits of my classmates for $10. This was in 1961. I wanted to go to an art college in the worst way but my Dad insisted I get a liberal arts degree and teach English "to be able to have security in my life." I didn't make it in the University and ended up in a 3-year commercial art school where I got mostly straight A's.

I learned graphic arts and went into advertising and publishing, became a creative director and had a pretty good career. But I disliked it intensely. I wanted to paint in the fine art field but was throwing my whole self into my job and the demanding time restraints of deadlines and long overtime hours. In 1986 I had some kind of a nervous breakdown and wasn't able to work for almost a year. At the end of that year I moved and started a new life as a mural and portrait painter.

By 1991 I had my own business and didn't know a thing about running it. My days became consumed with looking for projects and selling my existing work for peanuts to pay a bill or buy food. However, the stress of not having a steady paycheck seemed a lot less painful than the jobs I had had with publications.

Even though I knew nothing about marketing, I learned how to generate work on my own, I got my drawings and painting into juried shows, I met a lot of people and networked, finding those that wanted portraits or murals painted. I also found collectors that bought a lot of my work. However my ability to price my own work or see value in it was not getting better with experience. On mural jobs I would determine a price I thought would cover everything but in the end I always took a loss because I took too long or had to pay too much to an assistant.

Learning the different materials used in mural painting was also a challenge and I made many mistakes. I was better at trouble shooting than completing a project correctly and on time. Or maybe I underestimated the time it would take and caused unrealistic expectations from my client. Whichever it was, it made every job more difficult. The up side of all this is because of my technical ability the end result would look very accomplished and most of the time the client was pleased. I can count on 2 fingers the number of projects or portraits that ended in complete disaster that could not be resolved.

I was hired to paint two corporate murals with which I taught high school seniors on one of them to assist me and inmates at the county jail to assist me on the other one. I no longer paint murals though, because physically I can't climb a scaffold without special equipment. Now I do still paint portraits in oil, pastel, watercolor or charcoal. I went back to school a few years ago and took an Illustration class for one semester and a watercolor class for 4 semesters. I illustrated 3 books since then and have sold a dozen of my watercolor flowers and landscapes. I sell my watercolors for $500 each and my oils, portraits and landscapes for any price up to $5000.00.

I have not produced anything new in watercolor for about 2 years. I do continue to paint portraits and landscapes on commission and to show the watercolors I have not sold yet. And I recently produced a pastel portrait that I have been wanting to do for years from a photo I took. When I sent it around to my email list I got a very nice oil portrait commission that I am now working on. (But for a very low price).

A month ago I put together all the money I had left over from a large landscape I painted for $5000.00, in the beginning of this year, and took a master portrait workshop. It was the first time I had formal instruction in oil painting and portrait painting. I made it happen because I was convinced that he had the secret formula that has been missing in my work all these years. I do feel better armed now with more knowledge of how to paint a portrait from a live sitting. It remains to be seen if I am going to transform as a painter from that one workshop, which is the expectation I had put on it.

As to other challenges, I seem to sabotage myself by getting distracted by every phone call from friends and family. I spend a lot of time also doing projects for trade or to pay back a debt and *then get overwhelmed by the reality of the size of the project. I now owe three pieces to people who have already given me either a loan or trade in professional service. I have in the past painted close to two dozen portraits to pay people back and know I will get to these last three at some point but they weigh on my mind constantly.*

I feel deep down that I do all these things to avoid painting what I really want to paint, but I don't know why I do it. I am still not able to price my work or get a price I really want. I'm still financially in the hole even though I have quite a few collectors and repeat customers. But they don't come consistently enough for me to stay afloat and again, I don't get paid nearly enough to keep me going. I will go for several months with nothing coming in and it seems to drag me down to where I can't get a momentum going to make more images during my down time.

My own negative thoughts about my choices for subject matter stop me from moving forward. I tell myself those ideas are not important enough. Or what I am attracted to or desire to paint is not a winning choice. I don't understand why I talk myself out of doing what I desire to do the most? I'm not afraid to take risks in other areas of my life or on my projects, but with my lifelong dream I seem to be afraid.

I was recently diagnosed with ADHD. This is something that is prevalent in my family, but I never considered that I had it. It does explain a lot to me about why I have problems retaining what I read or why my mind wanders frequently. And why at the end of the day I feel like I haven't accomplished anything even though much has been done. When I'm painting the racing thoughts stop and time stands still, I'm not cognizant of my physical being and don't notice if I am hungry or thirsty. When I finish a piece of art I feel great about myself. I feel relaxed and less anxious. And yet I have a resistance to finishing. I love starting a piece of art but then I abandon it for days or weeks before I work on it again.

My minimum goals are these: Map out a time schedule that I can follow and stick to and track my progress. Have definite hours in which I do not answer my private calls, watch TV or look at my email. Maybe figure out a side business (such as selling prints of my work, teaching private classes, or painting more quick watercolors) that could give me a consistent income that doesn't take all my time and energy but gives me more control over my finances and gets me organized. My maximum goals are these: Find out what I most love to paint and make it my creative identity. In my daydreams I want to paint certain images and series, get them into galleries and become an established artist. (Not too lofty, is it?) :))

Thanks, Claire

**

Hi, Claire:

I'd like us to work on the big goals first <smile>. Although I know it is difficult and awkward to do, can you say in words what those images and series are that you want to paint? You also say that you would love to find out what it is you most love to paint: can you explain to me how you might go about "finding out" <smile>? What would that exploration look like?

Best, Eric

**

There are several series in the works right now. One of them is a series of images from my childhood. They are all about me and my caregiver parents. I have one completed image and one started. I have maybe five or six planned. They are very contemporary and include objects from my past. The completed painting is a black and white canvas with me when I was five years old, standing there in my little leather booties that I had to wear back then. I've nailed a pair of 1960's Flying Ace roller skates to the canvas and hooked them in the front. The title is "My First Pair of Skates". I've shown this painting in three gallery shows between Los Angeles and Baltimore.

I had planned to extend the series with images of other disabled people but I've only done five of those so far. Two of those have shown in a gallery and two of them are not working as well as I had hoped. Finding the people to pose for this very sensitive subject is the biggest challenge. I'm still not sure if these paintings are better reserved for specialized venues as opposed to any public gallery.

The second series is of people I know that I would like to paint for one reason or another. I already have quite a collection of photos of them. This idea to just paint people I know and expand their character into a personal story came to me when I was in a gallery and saw two portraits by Jerome Witkin. I was struck by how he had captured them in such a way that I felt like I personally knew them. It was powerful.

The rest of his paintings were extremely memorable in that they all had strength and power in the lines, the structure and the content. I do love paintings that are narrative as well. The images for these would be harder to describe beforehand because they would happen during the painting session with each person. But I believe in order for them to be important they would have to speak to the viewer in a personal way as well.

People are my first love. I have always been drawn to people, to character, to style and lifestyle. People fascinate me. The more people I meet, the more I want to paint them. I find myself studying their features, the shadows, the light on their faces while we are talking. I think that is what I am most drawn to. I have a very large file of photographs of people that have agreed to sit for me and let me paint them. I work a lot from photos but working from life is really the most authentic way to study the light and the energy they embody. I won't say "aura" or "soul" because I have never seen anyone paint someone's soul, for real.

How would I go about finding out what I love the most? When I think about it, what I think about the most seems to be this series of portraits of people that I know. Maybe I need to find the feeling of passion. Painting commissions wears me out and I have no energy left. I want to stop painting commissions (eventually when I can afford it). That's another goal. :))

Thanks, Claire

**

Hello, Claire:

Well, let us keep it simple for the coming two weeks, shall we? Why don't you pick one of your projects, the one that you currently feel the most passionate about, and approach it with exactly that passion—approach it as if you were in love with it <smile>! Shall we let that be our two-week goal?

**

TWO-WEEK REPORT

Predictably, two weeks just flew by and I found myself staring at my calendar that said I needed to make my two-week report to you today. Here's what I did do towards my goal of creating a series of paintings:

Started a morning ritual of getting up and meditating for fifteen minutes and reciting a grateful list. I do that every morning now for the past ten days. First ritual I've ever stuck with. Ever. It gives me energy and I start the day with a positive outlook. Plus I'm getting the habit of sticking to something that I'm committed to.

Make a daily structure list right after meditating ... haven't actually started that one yet but it's next.

Made a list of specific paintings that I would like to start with. It feels small to me since I only came up with five and I know there are a lot more flying around in my head.

I have a large white piece of canvas (60" x 75") stapled to my plywood wall waiting for me to paint something on it. I stretched it and gessoed it, sanded it and gessoed it again. I look at it every day and visualize what to paint on that canvas. I love painting large canvases so I thought I would start with that. But each time

I look at it I see a different painting on there in my imagination and I get stopped. I'm still not sure what to start with.

I made a plan to sit at my table and do some sketches of the different ideas I have because that might help me choose. It's a good idea but I haven't done that yet.

I did complete one portrait painting that I wanted to do for my own reasons. I consider that an accomplishment against all odds. Almost completed a commission that I have been working furiously on because I need the money to pay my bills. I am in serious trouble right now because several pieces of work I was expecting have not come in yet and I can't seem to focus on anything else but what is not happening. When this happens I don't put passion for art in front of my basic needs to keep my apartment, eat and feed my cats. Whenever I'm working on a commission during desperate times, all my energy goes into that painting and my focus is on not having any money. Even though I know that thinking this way is counterproductive I can't seem to stop doing it this way.

Last but not least I've been having a very hard time emotionally lately. I suffered a very bad break up a month ago that has put me all the way back to 1990 when my last bad break up happened. Only that time I couldn't function for months. This time I just kind of spend the days walking in between the bewilderment and the pain.

Every day I find myself getting depressed but I talk my way back up. That alone takes quite a bit of energy but I keep going because my art is my gift and I'm not going to let another person stand in the way of that. My friends support me in what I'm doing and I'm very lucky to have as many friends and family members that are on my side. Without them I would be nowhere.

So far, that's what is going on with me. I'm getting a lot out of writing these things down and being aware of my daily activity. So thanks.

Best, Claire

**

Hi, Claire:

So sorry to hear about the break-up! Those events matter and we have to take them into account, just as we have to take into account other real matters like needing money and having to survive. Given all that was going on for you during the part few weeks, you have done really well!

I think that I would suggest for the next three weeks that you continue taking care of your basic emotional and financial needs as best as you can while at the same time "biting the bullet" and tackling a blank canvas or two. A blank canvas and what we see in our mind's eye are of course "perfect" but we have to let ourselves move from that perfection to the reality of painting, whatever that reality brings. So "be real" <smile> and begin to work on those blank canvases!

**

Is the elusive creative work that haunts us elusive because nothing that gets made is as marvelous as the feeling we had about how beautiful it would look, how much it would mean, and how greatly it would satisfy us? Are we made sad and even paralyzed by the fact that reality must fall short of our dreams? This appears to be true for many artists, who see in a blank canvas perfection and who have no heart to sully that perfection with the reality of brushstrokes. We are hoping that paint on canvas or words on the page or music in the air might amount to miracles! How high we set the bar, where human beings can hardly tread.

TIPS FOR COACHES AND PROSPECTIVE COACHES

What Is Coaching?

Coaching is simply helping another person. You draw on your life experience and your wisdom and you learn by doing. There is no other way to learn but by doing. That means that your first clients are getting an unseasoned you—but someone has to get an unseasoned you! Most coaching programs use the dyadic peer model: two coaches-in-training coaching each other. You can learn by coaching a peer, by coaching a buddy, by coaching volunteer clients, and so on: but you will only learn by actually coaching.

What else do you need, in addition to doing? Well, you probably need some basic principles and guidelines, about being of help, about being respectful, about working from a client-centered perspective, about providing support, about holding clients accountable, and so on. You need to think about what's transpired after it's transpired. You need courage; a helping attitude; compassion; and your wits about you. Those are the tasks of a coach and the skill set of a coach.

What is the work? The work is both helping clients with the issues they raise and also identifying issues they have not raised. How do you help? You ask clarifying questions that cause a client to think. You wonder aloud about whether a client might want to try x, y, or z. You offer suggestions. You propose exercises. You teach—maybe a cognitive technique, a breathing technique, or an organizational technique. You are "in it" with your client, using whatever you have in your human arsenal to help your client deal with her challenges and solve her problems. You are being of help. That is the work.

Coaching is helping a person with the thing he says he wants changed or improved. Maybe he can't say what it is he wants improved; then you help identify what's wanted. One tennis player may want to be coached on his backhand; another may "want to get better" and is hoping that you can spot where he can improve. That is, a client may come in with concrete issues ("If I could manage to write and sell my novel my life would feel much more meaningful!") or with a global, amorphous need ("I don't know what I need but I know that I've had problems with meaning since childhood").

With one client you so-to-speak work on his backhand and with another client you work on every part of his game. That is, with a client who feels that his main concern is getting recognized as a writer, you help him do exactly what he says he wants to do: write his novel, sell it, have a career, make his mark, and so on. You take him at his word and focus where he asks you to focus. With another client, you work on every part of his game, either because he has expressed that many things aren't working (his backhand, his forehand, his serve, his court movement, and so on) or because he can't name what exactly isn't working.

What is the actual work? Well, if a client says, "I think that if I felt more confident, stopped letting my mate walk all over me, finally gave my dad a piece of my mind, and got my painting career started, I would feel a lot better," you help her plan how she is going to feel more confident, stop letting her mate walk all over her, give her dad a piece of her mind, and get her painting career started. Your client has done a lovely job of explaining to you where she wants help; then you start to help.

Over time you hone your skills. These include your listening skills, your ability to empathize, your ways of being direct, your ways of holding another person accountable, and so on. There are many helping skills to hone over time, from problem-solving skills to skills of personal presence. These skills fall into two rough categories: skills that help you support your client and skills that help you hold a client accountable. You are both a cheerleader and a taskmaster and both skill sets require honing.

You deal with everything and anything except for those things that you can't or shouldn't deal with. You deal in a common sense way with all sorts of psychological matters but you don't "diagnose and treat mental disorders," whatever that phrase means. That is really the chief difference between coaching and psychotherapy. Coaches need to be psychological but we don't "diagnose and treat mental disorders." You also don't offer legal advice, medical advice, and so on. But you do offer lots of advice and suggestions in many, many areas.

What Does Coaching Look Like?

What is it that a coach actually does? Well, whether you're doing creativity coaching, life coaching, spiritual coaching, business coaching, or some other coaching, you will probably learn to do all of the following 24 things—let's call them tactics. These 24 tactics constitute the nuts and bolts of coaching. Let me run through them using two examples, one a writer named Jack and one a writer named Mary.

1. You offer an opening

This sounds like:

"Hi, Jack, very nice to be working with you. What's on your mind?"

Or:

"Hi, Mary, very nice to be working with you. You mentioned a lot of issues in your email to me – where do you think you'd like to start?"

2. You ask clarifying questions

This sounds like:

"Jack, you mentioned that you started three novels before starting this one. What happened with those?"

Or:

"Mary, you mentioned in your email that you hadn't completed any of your previous novels. Can you tell me a little bit more about that?

3. You interrupt to clarify

This sounds like:

"Jack, I didn't quite get that. Can you explain that a little bit more?

Or:

"Mary, you say that you have a quiet room with a desk but I think you just said that you prefer to write in the living room with a lot of noise all around you. Can you clarify that a little for me?"

4. You interrupt for emphasis

This sounds like:

"Jack, what you just said strikes me as important! Can we stay there for a minute?"

Or:

"Mary, I wonder if that rude rejection letter is what caused you to stop writing? Can we look at that a little bit more?"

5. You make suggestions

This sounds like:

"Jack, I have a suggestion. The novel of yours that you were just talking about, it sounds so near to completion, I wonder if it's time to maybe complete it? What do you think?"

Or:

"Mary, you know, you might try writing in a café if your husband and your kids bother you too much at home. What are your thoughts about that?"

6. You identify potential problems

This sounds like:

"Jack, you say that you want to start a morning writing practice but you also say that you like to stay out late. Do you think that the staying out late might get in the way of your ability to get up early and write?"

Or:

"Mary, you say that your in-laws will be visiting and that you have to entertain them a lot. Will that get in the way of your writing schedule?"

7. You clarify goals

This sounds like:

"Okay, Jack, it sounds like you'd like to complete that older novel before really launching the new one. Is that the goal, then, finishing that older novel?"

Or:

"Okay, Mary, it sounds like the goal is to be able to write regularly in the context of your busy, demanding life. Is that a fair way to state the goal?"

8. You plan and schedule

This sounds like:

"Okay, Jack, how many days during the coming week do you want to work on your novel and how many hours a day do you want to devote to it?"

Or:

"Okay, Mary, let's create a schedule that helps you keep writing while your in-laws are visiting."

9. You teach

This sounds like:

"Jack, you know, there are a lot of reasons why writers have trouble finishing their books. Let me share a few of those reasons with you and see if any of them ring a bell."

Or:

"Mary, let me share with you why I think it would be great if you could institute a morning writing practice. I think there are three important reasons for giving that a try."

10. You create a sense of solidarity

This sounds like:

"Okay, Jack, let's see how we're going to tackle this next challenge!"

Or:

"Okay, Mary, let's put our heads together and see what we can come up with!"

11. You cheerlead, encourage, and support

This sounds like:

"Wow, Jack, getting 5000 words done this week is great. Congrats on that!"

Or:

"Wow, Mary, actually managing to write while your in-laws were around is amazing. Congrats on that!"

12. You invite accountability

This sounds like:

"Okay, Jack, I want to suggest the following. If you're willing, I'd like to have you check in weekly via email on your goals. What do you think about that?"

Or:

"Mary, what are your thoughts on a short daily email check-in? You'd just let me know that you'd got to your writing or, if you hadn't, that you intended to get to it tomorrow. What do you think about that?"

13. You repeat and confirm

This sounds like:

"Okay, Jack, let me see if I've got this right. You want to get a thousand words done each day as you work to complete your novel. Is that right?"

Or:

"Okay, Mary, let me just double-check to see if I have this right. You want to try to write six days a week and then get in some painting on Sundays. Is that right?"

14. You check-in on goals

This sounds like:

"Okay, Jack, last week you set the goal of writing six days out of seven. How did that go?"

Or:

"Okay, Mary, you hoped to write for an hour a day despite having your in-laws visiting. How did that go?"

15. You reframe and offer alternatives

This sounds like:

"Jack, absolutely, you could look at self-publishing as a complete negative. But I'd like to point out a few positives to self-publishing."

Or:

"Mary, I know you're holding your in-laws' visit as a catastrophe but I wonder if there's a way we can look at it as an opportunity for you to learn how to write 'in the middle of things'?"

16. You focus on cognitions

This sounds like:

"Jack, I think I heard you just say that you're no good at public speaking and don't want to do book signings when your book comes out. I wonder if that's a thought that serves you very much?"

Or:

"Mary, you just said that you find it impossible to write unless you check your emails first. I wonder if that 'impossible' is really an 'impossible' or maybe something else?"

17. You focus on behaviors

This sounds like:

"Jack, you say that you have to read the newspaper and check online news before you get to your writing each day. Can you tell about how long you spend on that?"

Or:

"So, Mary, you say that when you get an idea you're not in the habit of writing it right down. I wonder if we can change that behavior and get you in the habit of writing down your ideas when they come to you?"

18. You ask for updates

This sounds like:

"Jack, you know, I haven't checked in recently about those blog posts you were hoping to get written. Want to catch me up on how that went?"

Or:

"Mary, we were also going to keep track of whether you were getting to your Sunday painting but I haven't asked about that for a while. How has that been going?"

19. You send your client out to investigate

This sounds like:

"Okay, Jack, since going to a writer's conference interests you why don't look into writers' conferences and report back on what you find out?"

Or:

"Okay, Mary, we're getting very close to having you submit to literary agents. Want to investigate the world of agents and come up with a list of agents you intend to submit to?"

20. You role-play and rehearse

This sounds like:

"Okay, Jack, so you're going to have your first interaction with a literary agent. What do you think about us role-playing that a bit?"

Or:

"Okay, Mary, you say that you're ready to tell your father to stop bad-mouthing your choice to write. Do you want to rehearse what you want to say to him?"

21. You express your worries and concerns

This sounds like:

"You know, Jack, I'm a little worried that you won't be able to keep to your writing schedule while you're traveling. Can we think that through and see if we can come up with some tactics for writing while you travel?"

Or:

"Mary, I'm a little worried about you suggesting to your in-laws that they stay another month. Can we look at how that might play out around the writing?"

22. You refer

This sounds like:

"Okay, Jack, if you intend to self-publish you'll need some-one to design the cover and someone to format the manuscript. If you go to the following website you'll find a lot of recommen-dations for formatters and cover designers."

Or:

"Okay, Mary, it sounds like we're in a territory that I know very little about. Who do you think might be the right sort of person to help you with this?"

23. You invite new plans and new efforts

This sounds like:

"Okay, Jack, we've tried a few things to get your morn-ing writing practice in place and it hasn't quite taken hold yet. What do you think we should try next?"

Or:

"Mary, it looks like you won't meet your goal of finishing your book by the summer unless we get some new strategies in place and unless we come up with a new plan. What are your thoughts on what a new plan might look like?"

24. You provide summaries and a sense of completion

This sounds like:

"Okay, Jack, this session we've talked about getting a morning writing practice in place, replacing some habits that aren't serving you with some more useful ones, and setting a daily word count goal. That's a lot! Congrats on all that!"

Or:

"Okay, Mary, for the past two months you've been working to fit your writing into your real life and you've managed to get an awful lot done! Congrats on that! How should we envision our work for the next month?"

Coaching really isn't fancier than this or different from this. You engage in common sense tactics that you believe will help your client identify her goals and achieve her goals.

How Do You Respond?

Let's say that you're doing some existential coaching, which is an interesting coaching specialty, and a client presents you with a meaning-related issue. Consider the following presenting issue and five possible responses that a coach might make.

Your client says: "I don't know whether it makes more sense to reinvest meaning in my writing, even though I've never been able to get anything published, or to invest new meaning in photography, which I think interests me a lot."

One possible coach response is: "Tell me a little bit more about your history with writing. What have you written, what efforts have you made to get published—tell me a bit about all that."

A second possible coach response is: "You say that photography interests you. I wonder, how do you usually go about distinguishing between mere interest and maybe deeper or more passionate interest?"

A third possible coach response is: "What if you were to try the following. What if you chose to write during the week and immerse yourself in photography on the weekends? How do you think that might work?"

A fourth possible coach response is: "What small action do you think you might want to take over the coming week to help you decide?"

A fifth possible coach response is: "You know, at the root of what you're experiencing may be the anxiety of choosing. I wonder if we could focus a little bit on anxiety?"

Let's give a name to each of these 5 characteristic coach responses.

1. The first we might call an information draw, that is, the act of gathering a bit more information. That sounded like: "Tell me a little bit more about your history with writing. What have you written? What efforts have you made to get published? Tell me a bit about all that."

2. The second we might call a clarifying question, with perhaps a bit of educating built into the question. That sounded like: "You say that photography interests you. I wonder, how do you usually go about distinguishing between mere interest and deeper interest?"

3. The third we might call a problem-solving suggestion, with maybe a little educating thrown in. That sounded like: "What if you were to try the following? What if you chose to write during the week and immerse yourself in photography on the weekends? How do you think that might work?"

4. The fourth we might name a call to action, in the belief that almost any action is better than passivity: That sounded like: "What small action do you think you

might want to take over the coming week to help you decide?"

5. The fifth we might call taking a useful tangent, that is, bringing up an idea of your own because you think it is useful or even crucial. That sounded like: "You know, at the root of what you're experiencing may be the anxiety of choosing. I wonder if we could focus a little bit on anxiety?"

Here, then, are the five basic responses: information draw; clarifying question; problem-solving suggestion; call to action; and taking a useful tangent. Try your hand at thinking about this. A new client comes to you and says that he's an unhappy architect and wants to be coached on moving from architecture to something more fulfilling. How might you draw out some more information? What sort of clarifying question might you ask? What sort of problem-solving suggestion might you make? What would that sound like? What sort of call to action might you provide? What potentially useful tangent might you take? Take a moment and give this some thought!

The Coaching Session

How might a session with a client start? Here are eight common approaches and all are perfectly sound.

1. "Hi, Gloria, why don't you catch me up a bit on what's been going on these past two weeks?"

2. "Hi, Gloria. Where would you like to start today?"

3. "Hi, Gloria. I thought we might start with what you wrote me last week about X. How did that play itself out?"

4. "Hi, Gloria. I think we ended our last chat focusing on X and you were going to try Y. How did trying Y work out?

5. "Hi, Gloria. I was wondering how that problem with X was going? What's been up with that?"

6. "Hi, Gloria. I was thinking about what we talked about last time and I had a question or two. Can we start with the questions that are on my mind?"

7. "Hi, Gloria. I can't wait to hear about X! Is that a good place to start?"

8. "Hi, Gloria. We've been focusing on x, y, and z. Want to catch me up on all three?"

However the session begins, the coach's goal is to get working. There may be an initial moment of pleasant chitchat but both client and coach understand that this session is precious time devoted to helping the client with his issues. The coach aims her client in this direction by using prompts like, "Catch me up a little on what we discussed last week" or "Let's start with you filling me in on how approaching gallery owners went" or "I think you were going to work last week both on organizing your nonfiction book and rewriting the first part of your novel—which do you want to start with?" The coach focuses her client quickly on the serious matters at hand without wasting time or flinching.

Each session proceeds in its own way according to what the client presents. In one session the client may be frustrated with himself and disappointed in his efforts and the work of the session may be helping the client forgive himself and recommit to the same goals he "failed at" the previous week. In another session the client may have made a lot of progress and may not know what to tackle next, in which case the work is carefully and sensibly choosing the next goals. In another session the client may want to meander and chitchat so as to avoid admitting that he hasn't done the work he said he would do, in which case the coach allows for a certain amount of meandering and chitchatting but sooner rather than later directly asks about the work, fully expecting to be presented with a sheepish confession.

This is a human interaction. Sometimes the coach listens; sometimes the coach coaxes; sometimes the coach teaches. However the coach operates, she dignifies the session with her humanness. She may have been trained to use a certain method or she may have come to the conclusion that she will adopt a certain method but in the end she uses everything she possesses in order to be of help, as no method really suffices. Once she realizes that a coaching session is not so much about looking professional but rather about being of real service, she can relax into the fascinating work of being with another human being who is trying to make some progress.

Sessions take twists and turns. It isn't that you do a certain thing for five minutes, another thing for ten minutes, and so on, but rather that, as in any conversation, you go back and forth and around and around in an effort to make sense of the issues at hand. You may start out a session checking in on how well your client managed to get to his screenplay and soon discover that you are discussing his desire to change careers, his longing to once again play in a band, or the fact that his neighbors are making his life miserable. A person's reality is made up of disparate elements like these and so is a coaching session.

Sometimes the two of you may get a little lost. What to do? Here are five things you might try:

1. "You know, Bob, I have the feeling that we should stop for a second and refocus. What do you think are the two or three things we ought to be focusing on?"

2. "You know, Bob, I was just remembering from the first email you sent me that you wanted to work on x, y, and z. Are we paying good enough attention to those issues?"

3. "You know, Bob, I wonder if maybe you could articulate one or two things you want to get accomplished in the coming two weeks. I think it would help me to hear what you have in mind."

4. "You know, Bob, we have a new month starting in a few days and maybe that's a great opportunity for us to refocus and recommit. What do you think you'd like to focus on in the new month?"

5. "You know, Bob, I've been meaning to ask you about X. I don't think we've touched on X in a long time. Does it seem worth our time to pay a little attention to that?"

Thus the coaching session proceeds. Probably a lot will get done! As you near the end of the session you will want to "begin to finish up" in the ways you have learned to finish up, perhaps by summarizing some key points. Coming to a sense of completion at the end of a session is a useful goal and you want to avoid as much as possible ending a session with a sense that there's some unfinished business remaining. The trick is becoming very aware that only a few minutes remain and to learn how to effectively wind down a session so that it ends well.

Naturally, you also want to steer your client to the work he or she is to do between sessions. What exactly are you asking your client to do between sessions? You might be asking him to do any of the following:

1. You might ask him to work on whatever it is the two of you decided that he would work on. For example, in session he might have mentioned that he felt ready to approach literary agents in the coming week. You agreed that was a great idea and the two of you discussed what he needed to do in order to effectively approach agents, maybe focusing on him strengthening the subject line of his query email and the body of his query email. Therefore at the end of the session you might say, "So, let me go over what we agreed on. In the coming week you'll work on creating an effective subject line for your query email, strengthening the body of your email, and figuring out which agents you intend to approach. Does that sound right?"

2. You might ask him to keep in touch with you about the progress he's making—or that he's not making. This might sound, "Okay, Frank, I know that you're going to try working on your first symphony this week. Please drop me an email when you get a chance and let me know how that's going—including any obstacles that may have come up. Okay?" Even if your client isn't officially paying for email coaching you might still sometimes make this offer of an email check-in.

3. You might make this check-in even more formal by asking him to check in with you on a daily basis. This might sound like, "Okay, here's what I'd like you to do, if you feel like it might serve you. Every day after you've finished your two hours in the studio, just drop me a quick email that reads 'Done!' I may not respond to your email or I may just say 'Congrats!' What do you think about checking in daily?" If your client feels that checking in that way serves him, then that becomes part of his work between sessions.

4. You might ask her to report on a particular event or interaction. This might sound like, "Okay, Mary, that editor said that she'd be in touch with you this week and we've rehearsed how you want to respond to the questions she's likely to ask you. Do you want to check in after you've spoken with her and let me know how it went? I'd love to hear! What are your thoughts on checking in with me via email after you've chatted with her?"

The session ends—but your client's work doesn't end. Part of your helpfulness as a coach is pressing your client to work between sessions on her goals, her dreams, and her aspirations.

Following, Leading, Interrupting and Inviting

During a given session you might do all of the following:

+ You might listen as your client tries to articulate his issues

+ You might ask questions to help you better understand what your client is getting at

+ You might help your client arrive at concrete goals

+ You might cheerlead and help motivate your client

+ You might single out something your client said because you consider it important

+ You might make suggestions and problem-solve

+ You might teach a little

+ You might come to an agreement about what your client will work on between sessions

As a coach you are both following and leading. Sometimes you will follow your client and sometimes you will lead your client. A client may frame a problem in a certain way and, while you want to support her way of framing the problem, at the same time you may believe that she is making a conscious or an unconscious mistake. She may believe, for example, that she is supposed to wait for inspiration before she begins her new career, an idea you might accept if she hadn't been waiting for this particular inspiration for three years already. You have the feeling that something very different is going on--maybe that she is too sad to begin, maybe that she doesn't believe that there are sufficient reasons to start this career, maybe because she is struggling too hard just to survive, and so on--and that "waiting for inspiration" is a way of avoiding looking too closely at what is really going on in her life.

How will you proceed? By remembering that you have permission to lead and by remembering not to be frightened of being real, just as long as you are gentle while being real. This might sound in your own head like the following: "I have no investment as to whether she will or won't begin this new career. In fact, I have my doubts that she will begin it and I don't want to get too attached to needing her to begin. But I would like to understand why she is having so much trouble beginning, and I would like to support her desire to begin. So I think that I'll ask her what's getting in the way of her starting, in addition to not feeling inspired. Maybe that will provide us both with some clues as to how we might proceed. While I doubt that her formulation about what is preventing her from starting her new career is on target, I will honor her formulation of the issue but also check in about what *else* she thinks may be going on here."

By checking in with her about what may be preventing her from starting her new career "along with not feeling inspired," you are subtly arguing that something else is probably going on. But you are not flatly disputing her formulation of the situation. By being careful and circumspect, you are likely to allow her to drop her defenses and to think more clearly and genuinely about the situation. You are leading, but not in a high-handed or aggressive manner. The subtleties of these dynamics can only be learned by monitoring how clients react to the responses you make and by noticing what helps and what doesn't help.

If you are a problem-solving sort of person, you may find it hard to follow and to accept your client's version of the situation. On the other hand, if you do not have much experience in leading others or if leading isn't your current style, you may find it hard to aim a person in a direction of your choosing. Whichever is more difficult for you, following or leading, work on that skill by leading more if you find it hard to lead and by following more if you find it hard to follow. Ultimately, both skills are required.

You'll also want to learn how to strategically interrupt. If you let your clients tell their stories without interruption--because you find the flow useful, out of politeness, because you're not sure when to interrupt, and so on—then you will need to present your stored-up inquiries when your client has finished telling his story. This can prove really hard if your client has gone on for a bit and there are now several things on your mind. Therefore regularly interrupting may be the better bet, especially if you've learned how to return a client to his narrative thread.

You can interrupt, ask a question, take in the information you receive, and return your client to his story by apologizing, "Before I interrupted, you were saying--" I think that this sort of "useful interrupting" is worth incorporating into whatever style of coaching you choose.

The following are among the sorts of useful interruptions I have in mind.

Your client says, "I've always wanted to compose, but I don't have anything musically to say--"

You might immediately interrupt and say, "I'd like to check in on that. What exactly do you mean by, 'You don't have anything musically to say'? I'm worried that speaking to yourself like that may be part of the problem!"

Maybe your client says, "I have several paintings that are done, maybe enough for a show--"

You might interrupt and say, "Do you mean that you do have enough paintings for a show or that you don't quite have enough paintings for a show? It wasn't so clear to me which you were meaning?"

Your client might reply, "Oh, I have enough paintings for a show but I can't afford the framing and I don't have good slides--"

Then you can say, "Oh, I see! That's much clearer. We'll certainly get back to this. I think you were saying before I interrupted you that you have several paintings done, maybe enough for a show--"

Sometimes you might interrupt, listen to your client's response, and then pursue what your client has just brought up, rather than allowing him to return him to his narrative thread. This might sound like the following:

Your client: "I couldn't just call a literary agent cold."

You, interrupting: "Still, is that a stretch you'd like to make?"

Your client: "No. It's too scary!"

You, now pursuing this thread: "But what if you were sufficiently prepared?"

Your client: "Prepared, how?"

You: "Let's talk about that. How does a person get ready to talk to a literary agent?"

Or:

Your client: "I just don't think I can speak other people's lines one more time! It's just too boring! I can't make myself audition--"

Your strategic interruption: "What about speaking your own lines? Is it maybe time to write a performance piece?"

Your client: "I've been thinking about that for the longest time."

You: "And?"

Your client: "I don't know. Those are different skills. I'm not sure I'm talented in that way--"

You: "But you do want to write a performance piece? Do you want to speak in your own voice?"

Your client: "I do."

You: "Okay, then! Let's focus on that for a few minutes."

Sometimes you interrupt because you need clarification or more information. Sometimes you interrupt because you want to take the lead and steer your client in a certain direction. Sometimes you interrupt because you want to educate or consult. The basic rhythm of a session, whether conducted in person or on the phone, is for a client to present her thoughts and for you to ask questions and sometimes to interrupt your client's answers with further questions.

If it isn't in your nature to interrupt or if it isn't a habit with you to interrupt, you may find yourself confronted by long narratives that contain so much unaddressed material that you have no idea where to begin or what to say once your client has finished speaking. It is a much better policy to interrupt a long narrative with intentional questions that allow you to coach as you go. In the sense in which I've just described, interrupting is an important habit to acquire.

Then there's the tactic of "offering invitations." Whatever style you develop, the technique of "offering invitations" is a useful technique to fold into your personal style. In addition to whatever else you do as you coach, you can always offer your client a certain sort of invitation. For example, you might invite her to try her hand at some things she might enjoy attempting that, for one reason or another, she is not currently pursuing.

Let's say that your client might well love to submit her latest short story to a well-known magazine but doesn't have the courage to try. You might invite her to try. She might relish studying a new painting technique but not have thought to learn something new. You might invite her to try. She might profit from turning her research into a nonfiction book but not know how to begin. You might invite her to try. You can invite her to attempt things which she has told you she would like to try and you can also invite her to try things that you independently think she might benefit from doing.

The following are some examples of invitations that you might offer to a writer client:

1. "Mary, I noticed that this month's *Writer's Digest* is devoted to writers' conferences. Since we talked about you possibly attending one, I thought I'd let you know. Care to take a look at the issue and report back?"

2. "Mary, I was watching the weather channel and noticed that you're starting to get some warm weather. Since we talked about you writing outdoors this spring, I wondered if you were giving that any thought?"

3. "Mary, you mentioned in passing that you had put aside a half-completed nonfiction book last year. I wonder if you'd like to talk about that? Should we bring that to a front burner?"

4. "Mary, I just remembered that you have a meeting coming up with a literary agent! I wonder if you'd like to role play and rehearse that meeting?"

5. "Mary, I just happened upon some inexpensive Internet writing courses that looked interesting. Would you like the link?"

6. "Mary, you say that you have a lot more research to do before you can start on your article. Yet you sound extremely well informed about your subject. I wonder if you could write a draft right now, using what you currently know?"

7. "Mary, I know that your publisher is looking for another romance, but I wonder if it's time to take a break from writing what no longer interests you and try your hand at the adventure novel we've been talking about?"

8. "Mary, I think you may be stymied in writing your historical novel by not being able to really picture eleventh-century Madrid. Would you like to spend a couple of weeks doing some research?"

9. "Mary, I just read an interview with a literary agent who claims to love representing exactly the kind of book you're writing. I know that contacting agents has seemed scary to you, but I wonder if you might like to contact this one?"

10. "Mary, I think you mentioned that you wanted to try a novel after you wrote your short stories. Now that the story collection is done, is it time to think about that novel?"

If you have an empathic understanding of your client's situation and inner landscape, you will naturally want to invite her to try out things that you know are already on her mind or that are just out of her conscious awareness and that she would love to try if only someone mentioned them to her. There is virtually no risk in extending these invitations and a tremendous upside, as your client may be thrilled to receive your one- or two-sentence invitation and may even be transformed by it.

Your Coaching Style

Naturally you are going to want to coach your way, in a style that makes sense to you and that suits your personality. Each coach brings his or her own style to the table and for most coaches that styles evolves over time, often moving from a so-to-speak aggressive problem-solving style—let's get your problems fixed!—to a more measured, collaborative approach that includes a lot of listening.

Here are eight characteristic coaching styles: the listener, the problem-solver, the teacher, the expert, the taskmaster, the peer, the friend, and the cheerleader. Let's imagine how a coach might speak to his client, Jane, who is trying to start an Internet business:

Here's how "the listener" might sound:

"Jane, I think that you're saying that you can't find the motivation to start your Internet business. Can you tell me a little bit more about why it's feeling so hard to get motivated?"

Here's how "the problem-solver" might sound:

"Okay, Jane, you say that the first step in setting up your Internet business is deciding about your website. Why don't you do a search and see if you can find half-a-dozen websites that you think work well and write down what exactly about them seems to be working."

Here's how "the teacher" might sound:

"Okay, Jane, starting an Internet business always has a lot of moving parts and the key is getting organized and staying organized. What sort of organizational scheme do you want to put into place so that you stay organized?"

Here's how "the expert" might sound:

"You know, Jane, the key to any successful Internet business is branding. That's the number one key to success. So tell me a little bit about what's unique about your brand?"

Here's how "the taskmaster" might sound:

"Okay, Jane, you said that you'd be able to spend three hours a day on your Internet business but that only happened on one or two days last week. Let's learn from what happened last week and let's set some new goals for this coming week, shall we?"

Here's how "the peer" might sound:

"Jane, when I started my first Internet business I found it especially hard to figure out what my website ought to look like and how it ought to function. Are you having those same difficulties?"

Here's how "the friend" might sound:

"Wow, Jane, what a hard few days you've had! That must have been terrible, hearing that news about your mother. No wonder you haven't gotten anything done on your Internet business!"

Here's how "the cheerleader" might sound:

"Jane, that's excellent news that you got in ten full hours this week on building your business! Keep up the good work! That's really great!"

Naturally your style will evolve over time. Each of us has a predominant style nearer one end or the other end of the directive/non-directive continuum. The very directive person is typically in a hurry to problem-solve. The very non-directive person is reluctant to offer suggestions, teach, or try out assignments. An effective coach combines elements of directive and non-directive coaching, being brave enough to risk making suggestions and ego-less enough to just listen. You may want to keep track of your evolving style by monitoring the emails you send to your clients and thinking through what your responses say about the style you're cultivating.

Your Five Goals As A Coach

Your first goal is trying to be of help. There are countless strategies and tactics you can employ in order to be of help. You can make suggestions, offer opinions, explain what has worked and what hasn't worked for you, provide exercises and homework, focus on some area that you think is particularly important, and so on. The main point to keep in mind is the simple-sounding but profound idea that you mean to be of help.

Your second goal is to not attach to outcomes. You want to detach from outcomes and expectations, making sure not to get invested in your client's dramas. You want to provide your client with the genuine freedom to go where he or she needs to go. This is not the same thing as having no stake in the process. The stake you have is your obligation to be present and to try your best to be of help. But you cannot make another person do anything—write her novel, create meaning, get ahead at work, and so on. Only she can do those things. You cannot have as *your* goal that she complete her novel or make a job change: only she can have such goals.

Your third goal is to try to understand. If we're listening well we understand when a person is sounding afraid, down on herself, overwhelmed by current circumstances, unmotivated, and so on. We also understand what to suggest in such circumstances, if we think about it. We can suggest a small thing to try, a belief or behavior to begin to change, and so on. If you really don't know how to think about the situation, then you ask your client to tell you more. As she tells you more, answers may come to her or they may come to you. This is the process of understanding.

Your fourth goal is to show support and to actually *feel* supportive. This might sound like "That sounds hard!" or "That was excellent work you did this week!" What can get in the way of you supporting another person? It might be that you're too adamant about the "right way" things should be done. It might be your inability to get out of your own shoes and see the world through another person's eyes. It might be your bitterness about not having been supported enough yourself. When you don't feel supportive, that may mean that your client is being pointedly difficult or it may mean that some shadowy thing has cropped up in you. Your main personal work as a coach may be to so-to-speak "soften" into a genuinely supportive person.

Your fifth goal is to be real. When you are pretty certain that your client is misinformed about something or has misconstrued something, you want to have internal permission to tell her what's on your mind. You will need to say this very carefully, as any difference of opinion can--and usually does-

-feel like criticism. But if, for example, she believes that she can find a literary agent to handle her poetry, when literary agents do not handle poetry, you will want to find the way to reality-test and speak the truth. This is also the area where you bring in accountability. Being real means reminding clients that they agreed to do this or that: and so you make it your business to check in on your client's efforts in a non-critical, supportive, but firm way.

If you decide to coach creative and performing artists, you would then have a sixth goal: to understand their particular issues and to develop strategies for helping that particular population. You'll have noticed that, in the coaching interactions I presented in this book, all of the following issues surfaced: sadness, anxiety, frustration, disappointments, uncertainty about what to create, why to create, and how to create, difficulties in getting to the work, doing the work, and selling the work, painful existential questions about meaning, resistance to planning, scheduling, and concrete goal-setting, and countless practical and emotional challenges, from chronic illness to chronic poverty to caregiving duties to personality shortfalls. Clients with these issues await you <smile>! And it is wonderful work.

I hope that this book has helped demystify coaching and given you some insights into what clients bring to the table and how one coach attempts to respond to clients. I've written a great deal more about coaching in books like *Coaching the Artist Within* and *Making Your Creative Mark* and I invite you to look at some of my other books if you'd like to learn more about coaching and artists' issues. If you'd like to get in touch with me feel free to do so as ***ericmaisel@hotmail.com***. And please visit me at ***http://www.ericmaisel.com***.

Whether you're a creative or performing artist, a coach, or a prospective coach, good luck to you!

CPSIA information can be obtained at www.ICGtesting.com
Printed in the USA
LVOW10s2339290614

392251LV00024B/892/P